Praise for

THE FIRST FIVE YEARS

"There are lots of resources out there on strengthening a rocky marriage or bringing romance back into it once the spark is gone—but I'm convinced that with the right newlywed foundation, we could avoid so much of that heartache in the first place! From communication to career, from intimacy to income, THE FIRST FIVE YEARS mixes wisdom with real-life stories to help young marrieds build a foundation that will last for the rest of their lives."

—Shaunti Feldhahn, bestselling author of *For Women Only: What You Need to Know About the Inner Lives of Men*

"Bill and Pam have relationships figured out. I wouldn't be having them back on *Marriage Uncensored TV* if I didn't think so. If you are a newlywed and you want your marriage to start strong and then to last long, this book is a read-and-apply necessity."

—Dr. Dave Currie, family coach, *Marriage Uncensored TV*

"This book is a blueprint for building a healthy, intimate marriage. It's relevant and practical and will give any marriage the tools to develop a passionate, intimate relationship for the long haul."

—Jim Burns, PhD, president of HomeWord, author of *Creating an Intimate Marriage* and *Confident Parenting*

"The Farrels, like us, care about helping marriages succeed. To start your marriage off well and give it a strong foundation, read THE FIRST FIVE YEARS and give it as a wedding present to every couple you know."

—Claudia and David Arp, MSW, authors of the 10 Great Dates series

"I have used Bill and Pam Farrel's material for many years now in ministry and my marriage. Their books have had a great impact on my life and I highly recommend them!"

—Tom Hall, president of Insurance Marketing Services,
LLC, Encinitas, CA

"Pam and Bill have a way of helping newlyweds truly understand and enjoy commitment. Every couple would benefit from their wisdom."

—Estha Trouw, *San Diego News* anchor

"Thank you, Bill and Pam, for this book! What an encouraging, funny, and practical read for a newlywed. The Farrels' honest and candid approach to understanding relationships is something that anyone interested in the opposite sex can understand. . . . I understand my wife more and can learn how to love her in new ways because of Bill and Pam's insights."

—Chad Eastham, author of *The Truth about Guys*
and speaker for Women of Faith's REVOLVE Tour

The
First Five
Years

Make the Love Investment
That Lasts a Lifetime

Bill and Pam Farrel

New York   Boston   Nashville

Unless otherwise indicated, Scriptures are taken from the HOLY BIBLE: NEW INTERNATIONAL VERSION®. Copyright © 1973, 1978, 1984 by International Bible Society. Used by permission of Zondervan Publishing House. All rights reserved.

Scriptures marked NKJV are taken from the NEW KING JAMES VERSION. Copyright © 1979, 1980, 1982, Thomas Nelson, Inc., Publishers.

Scriptures noted NASB are taken from the New American Standard Bible®, Copyright © 1960, 1962, 1963, 1968, 1972, 1975, 1977, 1995 by The Lockman Foundation. Used by permission.

FaithWords
Hachette Book Group USA
237 Park Avenue
New York, NY 10017

Visit our Web site at www.faithwords.com.

Printed in the United States of America

First Edition: September 2007

10   9   8   7   6   5   4   3   2   1

FaithWords is a division of Hachette Book Group USA, Inc.
The FaithWords name and logo is a trademark of Hachette Book Group USA, Inc.

Library of Congress Cataloging-in-Publication Data
Farrel, Bill, 1959-
    The first five years : make the love investment that lasts a lifetime / Bill and Pam Farrel. — 1st. ed.
        p. cm.
    Summary: "The first five years of marriage can make or break a couple, but this valuable resource offers readers the tools they need to build a love that lasts a lifetime."—Provided by the publisher.
    ISBN-13: 978-0-446-57997-1
    ISBN-10: 0-446-57997-1
  1. Marriage. 2. Marriage—Religious aspects. 3. Man-woman relationships. 4. Man-woman relationships—Religious aspects. 5. Spouses—Psychology. I. Farrel, Pam, 1959- II. Title.
    HQ734.F253 2007
    248.8'44—dc22   2007004368

To all who gave us the GIFT of a strong foundation
and a love to look forward to:

The ministry of Campus Crusade for Christ
Calvary Bible Church
Biola University and Talbot Seminary

To our own newlywed kids, Brock and Hannah:

May the GIFT of each other these first five years
be a GIFT to your future as well as the
GIFT of blessing and strengthening others' love lives.
Your love is a light.

Contents

Part One   **Get in the Game**

You Can't Make Up Your Own Rules
for Relationships, So Here's the Playbook

Part Two   **Invest in Great Sex**

Everything Looks Better After Sex

Acknowledgments

Many thanks to all who made this book possible.

To Tom and Barbara Buck: your love and care for us early on modeled a lifelong love to look forward to. We are who we are because you helped us learn.

To Bill and Tina Wilcox and Cal and Faith Myatt: Thank you for challenging us to make wise choices so early in our love. Cal, we'll thank you again when we get to heaven.

To the Conways: Jim, You have been an incredible mentor through the years. We pray many millions more will learn and benefit from all your relationship wisdom. Sally, your investment was invaluable and, like Cal, we will thank you in person when we cross the threshold of heaven. Jan, we are so excited for your new future with Jim. Thanks for being such an encouragement to him and for embracing us.

To Chip McGregor: Thanks for the writing opportunity, the inspiration, and for being a model of a man who lived the GIFT of investing well during the first five years—and now you and Patti have a lasting love. We value your friendship.

To Lee Hough and Alive Communications: Thank you for your dedication to this project and your wisdom.

To Holly Halverson: Thank you for your diligence, talent, and grace as an editor.

To the Hachette team: Thanks for believing in a book that millions need each year—you all are a gift to the world.

To the Farrel Communications staff, especially Debe, Jan, and Robin: Thanks for lifting the load so we could focus on writing.

To our kids, Brock and Hannah, Zach, and Caleb: Thanks for your patience and understanding—deadlines don't always land at convenient times. Your flexibility and prayers are a gift to newlyweds worldwide that you don't even know.

To Friends of Masterful Living: Thanks for all your prayers, love for our family, and practical help in ministering to millions of marriages.

Introduction:
The GIFT You
Give Yourselves

We've written this book to help the two of you lay a foundation for a successful, satisfying, intimate, and delight-filled marriage that expresses God's purposes. These early years are critical. According to a University of Washington study by relationship experts John Gottman and Robert W. Levenson, it is during "the first seven years of marriage, [that] half of all divorces are known to occur."[1] Speakers on a *Focus on the Family* broadcast noted that 20 percent of all marriages end in the first five years.[2] In our more than twenty-five years as relationship specialists, we have noticed a very obvious trend: couples who engage in premarital counseling, then follow up with a weekly study on marriage, have strong marriages that do not break up, no matter the external pressure or circumstances.

So laying a strong foundation is a very wise choice in the early years! It should be common sense that investing in your marriage early will mean blessings and benefits down the road. If you work on your relationship during these critical years together, you create patterns of living and relating that make the rest of your life easier and more effective. The first five years of your marriage are the GIFT you give to the rest of your life.

The GIFT Program

In this book, we will examine four key areas that create the GIFT you can develop in these first years together:

Get in the Game

Invest in Your Sex Life

Figure It Out

Tough on Me, Tender on You

Get in the Game

Relationships run well if you follow the rules of the game of love. You can't just make up your own rules and expect that things will work out. Just as an athlete has to compete according to the rules of his or her sport, your love will work best when you follow the guidelines God set in motion. Getting in the Game, which we'll cover first, involves discerning God's dream for you as a couple, accepting your differences, coping with female emotions and men's egos, and capturing and connecting to each other's heart.

Invest in Your Sex Life

These first five years are the time to invest time, energy, and creativity in your love life so you can create a strong emotional, spiritual, and physical bond. These bonds will serve you well in the years to come as more and more responsibility fills your life. You will have the habits and memories in place to remind you how much you love this person you are working so hard alongside. We'll discuss how to have soulful sex, what men and women really want from each other in the bedroom, and how to guard this precious thing husbands and wives share.

Figure It Out

Decisions set the emotional atmosphere of your relationship. Every healthy decision you make together will cause you to like one another more and give you confidence that you really can work together to build your unique family. Every unhealthy decision swallows up energy and erodes trust. As a result, decisions on education, career, having children, buying a home, and so forth are more than just logistic moves to stabilize life. They are vital pieces of the puzzle that connect your hearts to one another.

We'll talk about how to relieve the struggle of decision making, putting together a home, creating freedom for intimacy, and the considerations required when you're thinking about "baby makes three." We've included lots of information to help you make decisions you can live with.

Tough on Me, Tender on You

Couples who have been in love for a lifetime are people who have said to themselves, *I will be tough on myself, but I will be tenderhearted toward my spouse.* Relationships thrive in an atmosphere of forgiveness, grace, and mercy that is accompanied by a fierce, individual commitment to personal growth. Here we will cover how to make conflict constructive, how to get to your spouse's heart, and how to fill in for each other's weaknesses.

Each chapter concludes with a section called *The GIFT*, in which we'll present easy exercises that help you apply what you've read. We've also added sections called *Unwrapping the GIFT*, where we will provide ideas to help you experience the love life you always dreamed of. You didn't get married just to carry a bunch of responsibility together. You got married because you love spending time together and you love the way you fill each other's lives. In these newlywed years, it is a whole lot of fun to create some memorable sexual experiences you can reflect back on when tougher times hit. It is like putting money in the bank for a rainy day.

In all, these topics and exercises form the GIFT that your first five years will create—if you choose to use them! We can assure you, from our experience and that of many others, this GIFT is worth every ounce of energy and will you can put into it!

So let's get started.

Part One

Get in the Game

You Can't Make Up Your

Own Rules for Relationships,

So Here's the Playbook

1

Living the Dream

We all enter marriage with a dream. When you said "I do" to one another, a brand-new creation of God took place. You might even remember some of the people who toasted the dream at your wedding. Some see the dream as practical: "To the bride: may she share everything with her husband, including the housework!"

Others see the dream as impossible: "Here's to you and here's to me, I hope we never disagree; but if, perchance, we ever do, then here's to me, to heck with you."

While others see the dream as blissful: "May your troubles be less and your blessings be more, and nothing but happiness come through your door."

Roman 15:6 lays out the highest aspiration of marriage: "So that with one heart and mouth you may glorify the God and Father of our Lord Jesus Christ." You as a couple have much in common with other couples, but no other husband and wife on earth are exactly like you. The ways you interact with one another, make decisions, plan your lives, communicate your values, and enjoy your time together are unique and ought to be treasured. You are a vital part of God's worldwide, history-wide plan. The dream of your love will bring glory to God because you two, and the love you share, are intricately woven into God's plan of love for the entire planet.

As you dream about your life together, you may be thinking:

- I sure hope we are one of those couples that are so cute and in love as they grow old together.
- I hope we have the opportunity to have some kids!

- I wonder if we'll live in our dream home.
- I wish for long, romantic strolls on moonlit beaches.
- I hope that together we can become financially independent and live a life of ease.
- We'll never fight!
- I hope other couples notice how in love we are and want what we have!
- I hope we travel to exotic, romantic destinations around the globe.
- Sex is going to be red-hot and happen every night!

You have probably figured out that some of these statements (maybe all of them) are unrealistic. Don't be discouraged, because you hold the key to unlocking your dream and every time you enjoy your love, you reveal a little bit more of who God is, because "God is love" (1 John 4:16).

The paradox is that so many couples think they are just ordinary. They act as if God created some husbands and wives just to be filler on earth while he works only with the special people who are visible and prominent. Nothing could be farther from the truth. Our own lives tell the story.

Ordinary Couples, Extraordinary Influence

Tom & Barbara

Tom and Barbara Buck appear to be a rather ordinary family. Tom had an ordinary career and they have raised an ordinary family. They have lived in ordinary houses and taken ordinary vacations. To most of the world, they are just another family among the rest.

On the other hand, I (Bill) grew up with a controlling, creative, fearful mom. My dad was a good man who loved peace and often avoided conflict to the point of passively responding to my mom's outrageous behavior. When I was young, my mom tried to socialize but her fears eventually took over and ran our entire family. We lived isolated with no family or friends, and we were not allowed to be involved with anything she could not control.

As the youngest child in the family, I concluded I could not argue with Mom and win. I had watched my brother and sister argue with my mom repeatedly, but they lacked the fear-energy she possessed and she overpowered them every time. Two weeks before my senior year in high school, my mom came up with a very unconventional plan. My dad, my mom, and I had gone on vacation for a week, then Dad went home. During that second week, my mom decided that she and I would live in that vacation town for my senior year, in a twenty-four-foot travel trailer that had no shower! To seal the deal, Mom enrolled me in high school and waited until the weekend to tell my dad!

She also decided that Dad would come to visit us every other weekend. You would think that, as a seventeen-year-old competitive athlete, I would have revolted and refused to run away from home with my mom. Instead, I numbly agreed to the plan.

You might think that having to take open-air showers would have awakened me emotionally but it didn't—even when the temperature dipped into the thirties in the winter! I had simply resigned myself to live a life with no voice and no strength to back my opinions.

Intellectually, I knew this was not going to be a good habit to carry throughout my life, but I lacked the emotional and spiritual strength to overcome the influence of a lifetime of practicing this unhealthy approach. That is, until I met Tom and Barbara. As a present to help us out with our seminary education, they offered to let us live with them for three months, rent-free. We were young, idealistic, and flexible so we accepted the offer. I thought we were living with them so we could put three months' rent into the bank to save for school. I was really there to watch Tom and Barbara in action.

They were my parents' age. They were engaged in a real relationship with Pam and me. Pam saw another wonderful model, like her mother, of a woman who lived out Proverbs 31 in her love for God and her willingness to work hard. I saw in Tom an example of a man who was kind, productive, godly, and courageous. He supported Barbara in her pursuits but was willing to put his foot down when necessary. Barbara was also willing to encourage us when we did what was right and confront us in areas we needed to grow in.

And she was normal! I saw a living example of a woman my mom's age who was guided by conviction rather than fear. I discovered at an emotional level that I could trust men and women who were peers with my mom. This may sound so obvious you wonder why I am even writing about it, but it was profound in my life.

Up until that point, I assumed that all women my mom's age would become irrational and all men my dad's age would back down at critical moments in life. There were things God had wanted to do in my life through my mom, but she was unavailable. There were characteristics in my life God had wanted to develop through my dad, but he hadn't learned the skills himself. Plan B was to use other men and women their age to encourage growth in my life.

As a result of that short three months with Tom and Barbara, I have developed the willingness to ask God to change me in the areas that I would have buried when I was growing up. I can work alongside women in ministry. This has become a critical skill since so many women are involved in service in churches. I can listen to people as they describe the obstacles that hold them back and demonstrate for them a realistic path out of the rut they are living in.

My mom used a lot of reverse psychology during my childhood. I often heard, "You don't have what it takes. You will never amount to anything." This was confusing because I knew she loved me and I couldn't understand why she would say these things. Since I've known Barbara, the internal voice of my mom has grown quieter every year and the truth of what God says about me is getting increasingly louder.

It still amazes me that some people who consider themselves so ordinary have been used by God so extraordinarily to open up so many avenues of growth in my life.

For my (Pam) part, I needed to see in action a man my father's age who was truly kind, caring, and calm (you'll see why in a minute). Watching how Tom gently served and encouraged Barbara gave me hope that I too could have a marriage that was the "happily ever after" kind. Tom's daily expressions of love toward Barbara and his affirmations toward me as a daughter bolstered my confidence that Bill and I could have the kind of long-lasting love they shared.

Bill & Tina

Bill and Tina Wilcox are not well known in most circles. They were serving in a campus ministry in central California when I (Pam) was attending junior college. I was an impulsive, spontaneous young coed tired of the way I was living. I had grown up in a home with a wonderful mom and an alcoholic father. He was an amazing dad when he was not drinking, but he would rage and become demanding when he was under the influence.

As a result, I never knew which dad I would encounter and I learned to distrust men. At the same time, I was trying to be good enough to earn his love and I transferred that over to my relationships with men in general. I moved from one boyfriend to another, usually with no time in between. I felt I desperately needed men but didn't trust any of them.

After yet another family crisis initiated by my dad's drinking, I determined I was going to change. I realized that way of life was crazy and I wanted to find something different—something better. That is when I met Bill and Tina Wilcox. Tina took a personal interest in me. She taught me the basic spiritual disciplines: how to have a quiet time with God, how to pray, how to share my faith with others, and how to walk in the power of the Holy Spirit.

Their impact was especially important as Bill and I started dating. Because Bill and I grew up in dysfunctional homes, we were aware that we really didn't know how to have healthy relationships. To head off the influence of our families, we both had to learn to be very deliberate in our decision making. Bill and Tina met with us and encouraged us to ask hard questions of each other, to pursue books, people, and resources to heal the holes in each of our hearts. Bill and Tina held us accountable to take those steps of growth, often checking up on our progress.

My Bill purchased a notebook in which he wrote questions. He was desperate to do things correctly so he created discussion questions for us to talk through key issues. We lived two hours from each other, so our "dates" consisted of weekend visits to each other's hometowns. Before we began the weekend, Bill would pull out his notebook and we would discuss the questions at hand.

In preparation for these weekends, Tina would review with me what it took to develop a healthy relationship. With her help, I formed convictions about how to dress, how to stay out of temptation, how to keep Jesus at the center of my thoughts and emotions, and how to choose my actions before I started doing them.

In many ways, we are who we are today because of these "ordinary" couples who discovered the GIFT in their first five years. Because they were committed to excellence in the lives God gave them, they were at the right place at the right time to have the right influence on us. In a very real way, this book is possible because of them.

You may feel you are an ordinary couple, but you also can have a supernatural influence if you are willing to accept your God-given purpose. Ephesians 2:10 says, "For we are God's workmanship, created in Christ Jesus to do good works, which God prepared in advance for us to do."

What About You?

We've seen that God works in couples in very specific ways. Some produce generations of pastors. Other couples are highly effective in business from one generation to another. Some couples quietly help others succeed in rather unspectacular ways. There are couples who are inventors, builders, actors, artists, and so on. The fact is that your God-given purpose has been developing for generations and it is now ready to be expressed through your relationship. God has been building this dream for generations and now you, as husband and wife, are intricately woven into His dream for the world!

STOP Throughout the book, we'll ask you to "push Pause"—stop reading and do an activity to help you better process the principles we share. Take a few moments here to work through the following questions as a starting point for discovering the unique purpose God has for your marriage.

- What do we do well as a couple?
- What don't we do well as a couple?
- What does God bless in a special way in our relationship? Why did Jesus bring us together?
- What does he want to accomplish through our life together?

The Dream: Find It, Fine-Tune It, and Fund It

Practicing the principles of the GIFT—the major investments you make in your first years together—will help you enjoy and express God's dream for you. Here, at the beginning of your life together, your adventure begins. It is now your privilege to find the dream, fine-tune the dream, and fund the dream.

Find the Dream
The dream is often elusive during these early years because you are still figuring each other out and your resources are relatively small. Your hopes are sky-high but you are living in a four-hundred-square-foot studio apartment. You have to make a weekly trek to a Laundromat. You each work a full-time job while you wrap up grad school. You live for the weekends so you can spend a little time together doing free things because the budget is so tight. Romance means renting a video and having sex on the sofa.

Your hot and fantastic nights of candlelight, music, and flowers are mixed with the mundane tasks of fixing the car and grocery shopping.

The good news is, finding the dream is usually low-cost: sitting entwined, talking for hours about hopes, dreams, and causes that you carry on your hearts. The trek for the dream is long walks at sunset, sharing the struggles of the day. The quest for the dream is lying in each other's arms and talking about what you love and want to try in the bedroom, and in the boardroom, of life.

Make time each day to talk. Commit to it. It can be twenty minutes over coffee in the morning, the drive together to or from work, or meeting for lunch if you happen to work near one another. It can be an evening walk and talk or workout, where you bike, canoe, or even skate and talk. The key is to talk every day. It is easy as newlyweds to get so busy pursuing the dream by working hard that you forget why you began the dream in the first place—to be with each other!

Fine-Tune the Dream

To fine-tune your dream, you will need to create and protect time together. You are a couple now, but many other people want your time and attention. Both your families want to see you and they are used to having a major say in the way you plan your life and spend your free time. Your friends grew accustomed to spending time with you and would like to continue to make memories somehow. Other young couples would like to develop friendships with you as they adjust to their new lives together. One of the keys to your success is to balance your priorities so each of these relationships gets the attention it deserves.

You're probably familiar with the phrase from the Ten Commandments, "Honor your father and mother." But newlyweds can get confused as to what that really means. You are a couple now, a new family, so you will need to make decisions to protect this new love relationship. Often the balance between couple time and family or friendship time can get blurry. Here are a few principles and ideas on ways to work out vital relationships in daily life that honor your marriage—as well as the other people in your life:

Honor means marriage first. In the book of Genesis, God made marriage a priority by making it the first institution He created. He also said that a "man should leave his father and mother and cling to his wife." It is terrific to have a win-win attitude and try to please all the significant people in your life, but in the end, if you are backed into a corner and forced to choose, always choose your marriage first, giving preference to your spouse.

As we mentioned earlier, the decisions you make set the emotional atmosphere of your relationship. We got introduced to this principle in a rather simple way on our honeymoon. We got married around Christmas and, after spending our first week alone, we traveled to Idaho for a second marriage reception and to spend Christmas with Pam's extended family. Everything was going pretty smoothly until we were preparing to leave for Christmas Eve dinner.

It was snowing and Pam asked the group of us in the living room which shoes looked best with her outfit. Her brother could care less, her sister and mom selected one option while I expressed another. Pam grew instantly stressed and emotional. I told her, "Honey, wear whatever you want. They are just shoes." But Pam couldn't see them as "just shoes" because now she had to decide whom to please.

A very intense ten-minute conversation (complete with newly-wed wife tears) ensued as Pam tried to convince me what a critical issue this was. After releasing on me the emotional pressure that had built up, she made the decision that calmed her down: she went out to her mom and said, "I'm ready to go. I decided to wear the shoes Bill likes."

This is a silly example—it was just shoes—but like all couples we had to learn to set boundaries in a respectful way. We have learned that this same principle applies to the critical issues of where you live, how you raise your kids, your plan to complete your education or the next step in your career. You need to be willing to accept advice from others who care about you, even seek out advice from those in your family and friendship circle you respect, but the decision is yours to make as a couple on how to apply the advice.

The primary goal is to balance family decisions so that you model for your children (or the kids you will have someday) the type of family relationships you want to have going forward. You may find that your family functions well when you connect with them weekly. Conversely, you may find that other family members try to control your behavior if you get together more than a couple of times per year. The key is to be deliberate, rather than accidental, about how you make family decisions.

The same goes for time spent with friends: talk through how much time you will spend with friends so that as a couple you are on the same wavelength on this topic, which will help you avoid unnecessary arguments. One principle to keep in mind is you will want to spend time with those people who have been, are, and will be committed to your success as a couple.

Honor means carrying out healthy family legacies and priorities. Many young couples think they are not honoring their parents if they do not always go along with the parents' plans and wishes. This is one of the quickest routes to insanity that we can think of. When a man marries a woman, at least two families come together (and sometimes more if there are multiple divorces in your sets of parents). This means a whole lot of opinions are flying around and, most likely, those opinions conflict with each other.

It is okay to say, "We will honor our parents by carrying out the positive values [such as integrity or a strong work ethic] they taught us, but we do not have to always agree with them on other issues." The way your family does things is not necessarily right just because they do it that way, so think it through. The way they do things is not necessarily wrong either, so don't overreact.

You will also have to decide, "We will not carry out the unhealthy patterns our families taught us." These might include using guilt to manipulate others, assuming responsibility for other people, trying to make everyone happy.

As you have already read, my (Pam's) dad was a generous man who did many things to care and provide for me, but he had a drinking problem that controlled much of his life. When Bill and I started having children, we visited Dad only when he was sober. Our kids never rode in a car with him if there was any evidence that he had been drinking. We decided to not have him babysit any of our children.

We also have a family member who struggles with mental health issues but has refused to get help. We have figured out that this person can handle having people around for only a few hours at a time before irritable, controlling, and irrational behavior begins. We spend limited amounts of time with that person. We have decided this is better than no relationship, but we don't want our kids to pay the price for someone else's refusal to grow. We want our kids to see us model that we don't write people off, but we don't accept dysfunctional behavior either.

One word of caution: if you are the first person in the family who decides to function in an emotionally healthy way, your family might not be all that excited because your good choices point out their shortcomings.

The same principles apply to friends. Some of them will applaud the changes that come when you get married while others will grow jealous, critical, or distant. Do not despair; just keep close to Jesus, keep loving them all by faith, keep growing in your life emotionally, relationally, and spiritually, and maintain whatever boundaries are necessary.

To fine-tune the dream, you must first protect yourselves as a couple—the dreamers. When you do that, your new identity as a couple, a family, will emerge.

Fund the Dream

When you fell in love and told your parents that you wanted to get married, what was the first question they asked you? Our guess it was the same one we had asked of us and the same one we asked our kids: "Can you afford it?"

Your life together and your dream as a couple must be supported by an income stream and a budgeting plan. It sounds so simple, but it is one of the most intense areas of a marriage relationship. Couples experience more conflict over finances than almost any other aspect of their lives. Deep-seated differences arise because people spend money according to their individual personalities.

We will discuss this in more detail in a later chapter, but here let us make the point that different priorities mean different spending habits. All of us want to have the things that are important to us. A husband may think a new truck is a must-have and a wife may think paying off a school bill is extremely important. You may agree on the importance of funding your dream.

If you have enough money flowing into your budget, you both will be happy. If, however, your budget is limited so that you have to choose a truck, the school bill, *or* funding the dream, you will experience conflict. For this reason, a budget is nothing more than an expression of your priorities. The question your budget will answer is, "Whose priorities will be reflected in the way we spend money?" You have four options:

1. You can agree on everything so that your budget reflects your shared priorities.
2. You can use the husband's priorities.
3. You can use the wife's priorities.
4. You can learn God's view of money and use his priorities.

The most stable of the four options is to adopt God's priorities for your budget. When your budget is working well, you can thank God for the success. When your budget is a struggle, you can take all the emotional turmoil that goes with it to God in prayer and relieve your stress with him, rather than on each other.

We'll talk more about this in chapter 14, but for now, get some financial tools so you can develop a plan that will enable you to fund the dream. There are some terrific resources available to help you accomplish this same-page thinking. Among them are Crown Financial Ministries and Ron Blue's books on managing finances.

STOP In the appendix we have supplied a simple budget worksheet, so if you have not yet completed this important document and talked through your income and expenditures, we encourage you to do so. It is a launching point for discussions that might save you some arguments. Many local churches offer small-group Bible studies that will walk you through all the facets of finances and help you come up with a plan you both can live with. There are lots of systems for organizing your finances, so keep looking until you find one that works for you.

Decide at this stopping point if you want to do the budget now, or if you'd rather sign yourselves up for a course in money management. The most vital financial decision is to decide to make financial decisions together. Your relationship will be all the better for it!

Follow the Dream

You are not God, so you don't have to figure out the whole plan ahead of time. You two cannot see very far down life's path, but if you step out, seek God, and ask him to reveal his plan, he will show you the right steps at the right times. As you follow, one step at a time, he will move you to the life purpose he has designed for the two of you.

As an example: we began teaching on relationships when we were newlyweds. We were young so we felt God wanted us in youth ministry. We began to teach on dating and relationship skills.

God didn't keep us in youth ministry very long. He directed our path to local church leadership where I (Bill) served as the senior pastor and Pam as the director of women. We again found ourselves teaching on relationships, this time to couples. We eventually taught those couples how to train their teens.

While our main focus now is married couples, we would not have gotten there without God leading us to teach on relationships to teens. The audience has morphed, but the dream was constant.

• • •

We've seen in this chapter that God has a dream for you but relationships and finances affect how much energy and money you can devote to each other and to that dream. Don't feel overwhelmed. As you obey God step by step, his dream for the two of you will unfold. It is an exciting adventure, and it is so much more fun to take the trek together!

 The GIFT

Where are you two right now in the dream process?

- Are you finding the dream? Then take the answers to the questions under the first STOP and write up a dream contract or motto. Ours would sound like this: *Our dream is to bring practical insights to people's personal relationships as a platform to reach every person alive with the possibility of a relationship with God.*

- Are you fine-tuning the dream? Are you protecting your new identity as a couple? What changes do you need to make in the way you relate to others to protect your new love?

- Are you funding the dream? Work on a budget and talk about why the dream is big enough and important enough for you both to stick to the plan.

Unwrapping the GIFT

If you do something romantic every day, if you invest time and energy to create a strong sex life, you two will develop a strong foundation for love and life. So let's start with something simple.

Place your hands over your spouse's eyes and ask this question: "If I were to yell, 'Surprise! Your sexual dream has come true!' what would you want to see when you opened your eyes? What would I be wearing, or what would we be doing?"

Take turns sharing, then do one or both ideas!

2

Men and Women Are Different—Accept It!

Two sisters decided early in their twenties that men were too complicated to make a significant part of their lives. As a result, they made a covenant to keep their lives man-free. They would not date, and they would keep all professional contact with men to a minimum. They were so serious about this commitment that they even extended it to their cat. They made an agreement never to let their cat outside just in case she met a tomcat and involved their lives with a male!

For twenty years, they kept their covenant. But then the older of the two sisters met a man who captured her heart. She tried to fight it but found him irresistible. He was, likewise, quite taken with her so he asked her to marry him. She said yes but wasn't sure how to tell her sister. She spent days rehearsing different ways to explain that she could no longer keep the covenant she had made early in life. She finally decided there was no easy way and just had a straightforward conversation with her.

Her sister accepted the decision but told her, "It is your life, but I think you are going to make things awfully complicated for yourself. As for me, I am keeping my side of the covenant. The cat and I will remain celibate for the rest of our days."

The morning after her wedding, the older sister sent an e-mail that simply said, "Let the cat out!"

We are sure this is not news to the two of you, but men and women are different—in wonderful ways! I (Bill) am very glad that

Pam looks like a woman! The first time I noticed her was at the swimming pool when we were in college. She had this cute way of walking on the diving board that stopped me in my tracks and caused me to take notice. I would love to tell you that I first noticed her heart for God or the way she prayed, but I would be lying. What I noticed first was the way she swayed on her way to diving in the water.

It sure would be nice, however, if Pam thought like a man. Now, don't get me wrong. If I had to choose, I would take her beauty with all the intricacies of her soul. But if God had asked me, I would have ordered her good looks, the cute giggle in her voice, and her big smile along with my decision-making style. It would save a lot of arguments and it would be much easier to get on the same page without long conversations or misunderstandings. But God did not ask me! He designed Pam without any input from me whatsoever.

I believe God wrote Romans 15:7 to everyone who has ever thought that redesigning one's spouse might be a good idea: "Accept one another, then, just as Christ accepted you, in order to bring praise to God." Two extremely important things happen when you aggressively accept one another. First, you release one another to reach your potential. Second, you cooperate with creation and thereby bring the praise of God into your home.

In the Beginning, God Made Them Different

In the beginning, God created man. His name was Adam, and they had a great relationship. They walked in the garden and shared the adventure of life together. Adam's life had purpose and spiritual vitality in the midst of a perfect environment. He was a remarkable feat of creation because he had been made in the image of God.

But Adam was only half the story. The image of God was too glorious and too big to be reflected only in a man. God had concluded that everything in creation was good: the sky was magnificent, the foliage was in full bloom, the animals were vibrantly alive. But man was not complete. And so God created woman. Eve came to a perfect environment and made everything better just by showing up.

In this great act of creation, God declared that men and women are the pinnacle of his creative efforts and possess equal value. God had plans for a great partnership between himself and the people he created. He would guide them while they subdued the earth and built a great society. But Adam and Eve took things into their own hands. They rebelled against God's plan and their hearts became corrupted. Men and women have been driving one another crazy ever since.

You have probably heard some of the following statements that reflect this frustration:

- What is the difference between a man and a savings bond? The savings bond matures!

- For Sale by Owner: Complete set of *Encyclopedia Britannica.* 45 Volumes. Excellent condition. No longer needed. Got married last weekend. Wife knows everything.

- To be happy with a man, you must understand him a lot and love him a little.

- To be happy with a woman, you must love her a lot and not try to understand her at all.

In our book, *Men Are Like Waffles, Women Are Like Spaghetti,* we summarized the differences this way:

Men process life in boxes. If you look down at a waffle, you see a collection of boxes separated by walls. The boxes make convenient holding places. Men's thinking is divided up into boxes that each have room for one issue and one issue only. . . . Social scientists call this "compartmentalizing"—i.e., putting life and responsibilities into different compartments.[1]

Men want to succeed in each compartment and will focus on the ones they perform best in. Because men can focus on only one box or issue at a time, they tend to see a problem as something to solve—not discuss.

Women, however, view things in just the opposite way:

> Women process life more like a plate of spaghetti. If you look at a plate of spaghetti, you notice that there are individual noodles that all touch one another. If you attempted to follow one noodle around the plate, you would intersect a lot of other noodles and you might even switch to another noodle seamlessly. That is how women face life. Every thought and issue is connected to every other thought and issue in some way. Life is much more of a process for women than it is for men.[2]

Women can manage many ideas at once. Problems are far more complex to them than they are to men, so solving the problem may not be as important as talking about it. But because women's minds are like spaghetti, with every noodle connecting to the other, multitasking is a joy and a breeze for them.

Note: one style is not better than the other. They are equal but different.

 Take a few minutes and discuss these two questions:

- What first attracted you to each other?
- What do you think is good about the fact that men are like waffles and women are like spaghetti?

Men Need Simplicity

A man's drive to succeed in his pursuits builds in him an intense desire for simplicity. Men like to dwell in "boxes" they feel successful in (and prefer to avoid "boxes" they do not feel successful in). To help us succeed, we long to be able to focus on one box at a time in life. We want a manageable schedule and evenly paced expectations. It isn't because the other areas of life are less important to us.

In fact, it is precisely because these areas are important that we must give them our attention. When we divide our attention, however, we begin to feel inadequate and the stress in life grows.

If we women value our husbands, we want to help them succeed, so we need to let our husbands do the things they need to succeed in and do them their way. So before you correct or make suggestions, ask yourself, *Will it really matter if he does this his way?* You might be surprised that often it doesn't. (For example, which route you take to the store: if his way works, let him drive!) A happy husband is one who feels valued, and he will feel valued when you give him the space to succeed by navigating key issues his way.

When it comes to projects, we like to work on them one at a time. I (Bill) can easily climb in a box and get immersed in the project. I forget that anything else is going on in my life as I lose myself in the work. When I can work this way, I find life to be very satisfying. When the project is over, I stand back and admire my handiwork. I usually find the people who mean the most to me and ask them to join me in the admiration. Every comment about the beauty of the finished product increases my sense of accomplishment. Every criticism of the process deflates my pride and makes me wonder if it really was worth the effort.

The quickest way to steal motivation from a man is to make him change focus rapidly. This is often confusing to women because they tend to process life in short bursts. They travel the spaghetti noodles of their thought process and actively switch from one subject to another. This makes for a fascinating journey in life, but when men have to switch subjects quickly, we get exhausted and confused. We lose sight of what is most important and have a hard time figuring out what needs to be done next. The reaction to this broad approach is we will often get angry or just walk away from what looks like a mess. While both genders like less-stressed lives, our paths to those uncomplicated lives are different. And one path is not better than the other—just different.

Women Need to Feel Loved

While men want simplicity, women long to feel loved. Men have a hard time understanding their wives' need to feel valued. When a woman senses she is the most important person in her husband's heart, all is good in the world. But when she senses that most other things are more important than her, she gets thrown off balance and is overcome with self-consciousness. A husband does himself a huge favor when he determines to remind his wife regularly of her value in his life.

Of course, men need to feel valued too. But their main priority is simplicity.

One man learned about valuing his wife in an unusual way. A homeless man was begging money off my (Bill) friend Jim, who was taking his wife out to dinner to try to make her feel special.

Jim said to the panhandler, "Sorry, I don't have any money to give you."

The homeless man looked at Jim's beautiful wife and said, "Whoa, if I had a wife who looked that good, I'd be broke too!"

As they sat down in the nearby restaurant, Jim looked his wife in the eyes and told her the homeless man was right about her being gorgeous. Jim then got out of his seat, went back outside, and gave the man twenty dollars. "Hey," Jim added, "I owe you a lot more than this, but I hope this helps." Jim had a great night with his wife as they rediscovered the way they make each other better.

A man who does not make his wife's value a priority may one day have an experience like this one: A woman accompanied her husband to the doctor's office. After his checkup, the doctor called the wife into his office alone. He said, "Your husband is suffering from a very severe disease, combined with horrible stress. If you don't do the following, your husband will surely die: Each morning, fix him a healthy breakfast. Be pleasant, and make sure he is in a good mood. For lunch make him a nutritious meal. For dinner prepare an especially nice meal for him. Don't burden him with chores, as he probably had a hard day. Don't discuss your problems with him, it will only make his stress worse. And most importantly, make love with your husband several times a week and satisfy his every whim. If you can do this for the next ten months to a year, I think your husband will regain his health completely."

On the way home, the husband asked his wife, "What did the doctor say?"

"You're going to die," was her reply.

STOP Each of you put together a list of things you can do to make your spouse feel loved. These things can be expensive like jewelry or tickets to a game, or inexpensive like giving a back rub or flirting. Or give a gift that will make his life simpler and her life less stressed, like a pack of Post-it Notes, a gas card so she won't run out, or a travel mug—anything that says, "I noticed you were stressed and I am trying to help."

The Hardest Question of All Time

Young King Arthur was ambushed and imprisoned by the monarch of a neighboring kingdom. The monarch could have killed him but was moved by Arthur's youth and ideals. So, the monarch offered him his freedom, as long as he could answer a very difficult question. Arthur would have a year to figure out the answer and if, after a year, he still had no answer, he would be put to death.

The question: *What do women really want?* Such a question would perplex even the most knowledgeable man, and to young Arthur, it seemed an impossible query. But, since it was better than death, he accepted the monarch's proposition to have an answer by year's end.

He returned to his kingdom and began to poll everyone: the priests, the wise men, and even the court jester. He spoke with all the members of his court, but no one could give him a satisfactory answer.

Many people advised him to consult the old witch, for only she would have the answer. But it would cost King Arthur, as the witch was famous throughout the kingdom for the exorbitant prices she charged for her knowledge.

The last day of the year arrived and Arthur had no choice but to talk to the witch. She agreed to answer the question, but he had to agree to her price first: the old witch wanted to marry Sir Lancelot, the most noble of the Knights of the Round Table and Arthur's closest friend!

Young Arthur was horrified. The witch was hunchbacked and hideous, had only one tooth, smelled like sewage, and made obscene noises. He had never encountered such a repugnant creature in all his life.

He refused to force his friend to marry her and endure such a terrible burden, but Lancelot, learning of the proposal, spoke with Arthur. He said nothing was too big of a sacrifice compared to Arthur's life and the preservation of the Round Table.

Hence, a wedding was proclaimed and the witch answered Arthur's question thus: "What a woman really wants," she answered, "is to be in charge of her own life."

Everyone in the kingdom instantly knew that the witch had uttered a great truth and that Arthur's life would be spared. And so it was, the neighboring monarch granted Arthur his freedom, and Lancelot and the witch had a wonderful wedding.

The wedding night approached and Lancelot, steeling himself for a horrific experience, entered the bedroom. But what a sight awaited him. The most beautiful woman he had ever seen lay before him on the bed. The astounded Lancelot asked what had happened.

The beauty replied that since he had been so kind to her when she appeared as a witch, she would henceforth be her horrible, deformed self only half the time and the beautiful maiden the other half. Which would he prefer: beautiful during the day—or night?

Lancelot pondered the predicament. During the day, a beautiful woman to show off his friends, but at night, in the privacy of his castle, an old witch? Or would he prefer having a hideous witch during the day, but by night, a beautiful woman for him to enjoy wondrous intimate moments?

What would *you* do?

Noble Lancelot said that he would allow *her* to make the choice herself.

Upon hearing this, she announced that she would be beautiful all the time because he had respected her enough to let her be in charge of her own life.

What is the moral to this story? If you don't let a woman have her own way . . . things are going to get ugly!

Silly joke? Maybe. Timeless wisdom? Definitely.[3]

• • •

We've seen that one of the most common sources of conflict in marriage is the desire of husbands and wives to change one another. To be sure, growth is necessary to maintain a thriving, loving marriage relationship, but this growth does not include changing the most basic aspects of who we are as people. In these vital characteristics we find satisfaction when we commit to accept one another "as is."

The GIFT

Select one thing off each of the lists you created and come up with a creative date that will make both of you feel loved in your own style. Create one day this week to do everything "his way" and another to everything "her way." At the end of the week, go out to dinner and share what you learned about each other.

Unwrapping the GIFT

Husband: Set aside an evening to enjoy one another. Begin dancing in the kitchen. Slowly work your way through the house toward the bedroom. At each room you dance through, take off one piece of her clothing. The key is to take your time.

Wife: Choose a day when you can be home when he gets home from work. Dress in sexy lingerie. As soon as he walks in the door, begin kissing him and taking his clothes off. Let the passion between the two of you proceed as fast as possible.

3

The PMS Roller Coaster and the Male Ego

Pam was bouncing around the house with a curious smile on her face. I was intrigued by the flirtatious way she was acting and starting to think it was going to be a good night. For about an hour the atmosphere in our home was as comfortable as I have ever seen it. Life was good and love was easy.

Then the air suddenly grew cold. Pam's attitude toward me became hostile and the freedom was gone. I didn't understand what had happened. She changed so quickly from an amorous, fun-loving wife to a sullen, distant, hard-to-understand woman. I could not comprehend what I had done.

I, in turn, saw a transformation in myself. I went from being so interested in Pam that I followed her around like Indiana Jones searching for valuable treasures to a disappointed, angry man who was feeling cheated out of a satisfying night of passion. All I had done was comment on her schedule: "Pam, I would really like us to spend time together tomorrow."

"Hey, Bill, that sounds good. Thanks for thinking about me."

"I'll be home around six. Could you have dinner ready?" Apparently, this question was some kind of a code for, "Pam, I take you for granted and the only reason I married you was so that you could cook and clean for me," because her eruption took me completely by surprise.

"That's all you love me for, isn't it? You have never thought my stuff was as important as yours," Pam shot at me with body language that could have stopped traffic on the freeway.

"Pam, I didn't mean that. I just thought we would—"

"You are always thinking about you! When is it my turn to be taken care of? I don't think you will ever understand!"

With that, she stormed upstairs. *Wow!* I just love PMS. The only thing that went to bed with Pam that night was my hope for the evening. I walked around the house fuming, sure that God had made a mistake when he created women.

The Weird World of PMS

We all know that PMS is short for Premenstrual Syndrome, but it could just as easily stand for "Pam's Massacre of Safety," "Pyrotechnic Monthly Show," "Perilous Mood Swings," or "Partner May Survive." It is that wonderful time of the month when everything is wrong and you become the beloved enemy of your wife.

Wife, you have PMS if:

1. Everyone around you has an attitude problem.

2. You're adding chocolate chips to your cheese omelet.

3. The dryer has shrunk every last pair of your jeans.

4. Your husband is suddenly agreeing to everything you say.

5. You're using your cellular phone every time you see a bumper sticker that says, "How's my driving? Call. . . ."

6. Everyone's head looks like an invitation to batting practice.

7. You're counting down the days until menopause.

8. You're sure that everyone is scheming to drive you crazy.

9. The ibuprofen bottle is empty and you bought it yesterday.

Husband, your wife has PMS if:

1. She stops reading *Glamour* and starts reading *Guns and Ammo*.

2. She considers chocolate a major FDA food group.

3. She's developed a new talent for spinning her head around in 360-degree circles.

4. She retains more water than Lake Superior.

5. She denies she's in a bad mood as she pops a clip into her semiautomatic and "chambers one."

6. She buys you a new T-shirt with a bull's-eye on the front.

7. You ask her to please pass the salt at the dinner table and she says, "All I ever do is give, give, give! Am I supposed to do *everything*?"

8. She enrolls in the Lizzie Borden School of Charm.

9. She orders three Big Macs, four large fries, a bucket of Chicken McNuggets and then mauls the manager because they're out of Diet Coke.

It is vital to keep your sense of humor when it comes to the hormonal challenges of the month, but we must never dismiss PMS as a trivial thing. There are as many as 150 symptoms that impact women and make them miserable. The most common include head-aches, backaches, skin breakouts, fatigue, depression, and cramps.

PMS: Whom Can I Blame?

Well, I (Pam) would like to blame it all on Eve and that "apple" she ate in the garden. It definitely is related to the ability to bear children and all those delightful hormones. Most researchers agree that it has to do with an imbalance of hormones during the second half of a woman's menstrual cycle. In a normal cycle, levels of estrogen (which stimulates the growth of the uterine lining, among other things) in your blood rise until you ovulate, then they decline and progesterone (which causes the lining to thicken) levels begin to rise. If your body is producing and metabolizing the right amounts of estrogen and progesterone at the right times, you won't get PMS.

But if vitamin deficiencies, emotional pressure, or any number of other stressors hit, *zing!* The delicate balance is thrown off and we women decide, *If I am miserable, everybody else ought to be miserable too!*

Most doctors recommend keeping a symptom chart so you have an accurate record of the emotional and physical symptoms affecting your life. It may be informative to rate your symptoms. For example, a headache could range from one to ten in intensity, ten being the highest. Your anxiety could be rated one ("I feel a little grumpy") to ten ("I feel as if I am totally out of control and want to hurt someone!")

Keep a record for two to three months to see if symptoms cluster around your period. If it's PMS, your discomfort should occur during the two weeks before your period and go away after your period starts.

I (Bill) began doing this during the second year of our marriage. In our first year, I was filled with compassion and felt like a hero whenever I was patient with Pam's mood swings. During the second year, I grew more cautious. Some conversations just made no sense to me.

"Hi, angel, how was your day?"

"I don't know why you ask, you don't really care."

"What do you mean, I 'don't care?'"

"You just don't care. If you did care, you would have asked differently."

"Differently? There are different ways to ask, 'How was your day?'"

"See, you are so insensitive. I can't explain anything to you because you never listen."

"I thought you told me you love the way I listen to you."

"Oh, now you are going to hold that against me."

You get the idea. It was like driving a car with no steering wheel. At first, I grew resentful of these conversations and spent a lot of time trying to figure out what I was doing wrong. When it happened month after month, I grew suspicious, so I began charting Pam's period on my calendar. I marked the ten days before her period as a "no-fly zone." During those days, I spent more time listening and less time talking. I put a moratorium on major decisions. I did all I could to lower stress.

Don't give me too much credit. I just figured out that our sex was better during the rest of the month if I protected the "no-fly zone"!

From All Sides

In any battle, the enemy needs to be attacked from all sides. PMS is no different. You are created with mind, body, and spirit, so the remedies should include many facets: adjust your perspective, identify your priorities, intensify your prayer life, and deliberately prepare yourself ahead of time.

Adjust Your Perspective

I (Pam) remind myself that millions in the world are in real pain. War, famine, and disease are real problems. PMS is just an inconvenience, for the most part. On my worst PMS days, I read biographies of women who have endured much and overcome much. On PMS days I send cards to friends who are ill or e-mail a friend who has just lost her husband or child. I refuse to sit around feeling sorry for myself, no matter how lousy I feel physically.

Identify Your Priorities

But I am also a realist. On the second day of my period, I always feel as if I have the flu. Everything aches. My head feels as if someone put it in one of those pump-up air football helmets, but they pumped it too full so my head seems as though it's in a vice. I give myself some slack.

I am not as creative on those days, but I can still do routine tasks: editing, research, housework, organizing, delegating. If I feel like it, I take a short nap, go for a walk, or swim. I have learned the exercises and activities that seem to lessen the physical symptoms and I add them to my schedule on those peak PMS days, even if it means setting aside some "vital" issue for a day or two.

Intensify Your Prayer Life

When I feel at the end of myself, I ask God to send His strength in the areas I feel weak: "God, I feel as if I want to snap everyone's head off. Give me your patience today. Please don't let me take out my pain on others. Instead, God, give me kindness in my answers, grace in my responses, and love in my expressions. I don't have it in me on my own, but because your Spirit lives in me, I know I can draw upon that power to do the right thing. Help me, Jesus." I don't want to say or do anything during PMS that I have to spend the rest of the month making up for!

Prepare Ahead of Time

I take life and its responsibilities down a few notches physically as well. If I have to carry a full load those days, I tend to feel exhausted, so I will say something like, "I am not feeling well today. I'd be more than glad to run those errands for you but I am wondering, can any of them wait until another day when I feel better?"

Sometimes they can, sometimes they can't. If the list is a must-do, then I make the deal that I at least get to choose the music on the radio.

You might benefit as well from educating yourself on some PMS options, consulting your doctor, and giving your spouse tips on what seems to help you the most—get him involved in giving you a little timely TLC.

On the Bright Side

Ladies, see what you think of this:

Is there anything good to say about PMS? One study indicates there is—though it hardly seems a fair tradeoff. A 1996

University of Texas, Dallas, study found that women with PMS show heightened awareness of their environment. They have better memories and a greater sensitivity to their surroundings than women who don't suffer PMS. (A small note of gratitude: This heightened awareness extends throughout the month, and not just during those few days when symptoms are at their peak.)[1]

While all you ladies are rejoicing over the fact that PMS makes you more aware of what is going on around you, we men are cringing. This means you see everything, remember everything, and carry the burden for everything. We are painfully aware that it is only a matter of time before we hear the glorious words, "Don't you remember?"

Guy to Guy

Keep one thing in mind, men. You signed up for this ride with her when you said, "I do"! Her issues became your issues. That is just the reality of marriage. Here are a few hints that help:

- *Get informed.* Learn everything you can about PMS. Sharing and caring equal connection to a woman. When your wife's heart is connected to you, she longs to offer you her body. Taking an interest in her monthly struggle is a great investment in your sex life! Sure, you will give to her selflessly, with no expectations, but when you show this kind of care, a woman spontaneously wants to give care back to you—and she knows what you care about the most!

- *Get a grip.* Women's emotions are erratic, even volatile at times, and you cannot allow her roller-coaster ride to determine your reactions. Just because she is in a bad mood doesn't mean you have to be in a bad mood. Just keep doing what is right and normal and give her some space. If she has a connection with God, God will whisper to her, "You overreacted. Go apologize." You don't have to point out all her mood swings and what might appear to you to be irrational thought patterns and behaviors.

- *Get stabilized*. Her changes and emotions can set off your unresolved issues and old baggage. If you've felt criticized or rejected by women in the past, you may overreact to your wife's mood swings. Resolve to be a mature man. Get a mentor. Meet in a men's Bible study.

- *Learn how to pray—alone, with your wife, and for your wife*. The number-one question we get when speaking to women is, "How can I get my husband to pray with and for me?" It doesn't have to be fancy. Just wrap your arms around her daily, or reach over and hold her hand, and pray something as simple as: "God, thank you for my wife. Encourage her today." Your praying voice is like music to her soul.

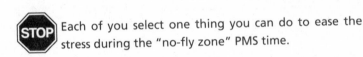 Each of you select one thing you can do to ease the stress during the "no-fly zone" PMS time.

The Inconvenient Male Ego

The male ego is just about as unpredictable as the roller-coaster ride of PMS. *Ego* has popularly been described as "Edging God Out," but it can also refer to "Easily Gets Offended" or "Every Guy Overreacts."

The first time I (Pam) noticed it in Bill was when he asked if he could kiss me. God had been working on me to wait until I was engaged to kiss another man. I had wrecked a number of other relationships because I am wired pretty hot. I loved the attention I would get from men I was dating and, before I knew it, the relationship was progressing faster and farther than I wanted. My mentor challenged me to interview couples I highly respected to see what they did before they were married. The common trend I discovered was that these couples had all waited until there was a commitment toward marriage before they kissed.

Well, the big night came. We had a very romantic dinner and walked under the stars. It was getting cold and I wondered why we were walking for so long, but I discovered later that Bill was building up courage. When he asked if he could kiss me, this is what I said: "I would really, really like to say yes, but I am wired very hot and I have pretty much ruined every relationship I have ever been in. You are important to me, and although I would really, really like to say yes, I am going to have to say no."

Bill just stared at me. He then drove me to my apartment in total silence. That was the longest twenty minutes of my life. The next morning, Bill picked me up for breakfast and explained, "Pam, I am really sorry about going quiet last night. I was embarrassed. I should have been the one to set the standard and I felt less like a man having put you in the position to decide this for us."

My first thought was, *Good, he is not going to break up with me!* My second thought was, *He felt less like a man? What is that all about? This is just what relationships go through and he is assigning all this male ego, macho stuff to it. I hope this is just a phase.*

Well, it is not just a phase. We were visiting an old family friend shortly after we were married and were dancing in their living room. Bill twirled me around and then ended with a big dramatic dip. At the bottom of the dip, he dropped me to the ground. He helped me up and then whispered in my ear, "Sorry, Pam. I just ripped my pants." I thought it was funny, so I said out loud, "You ripped your pants? Let me see!" I stepped behind him and sure enough, his pants were ripped open. I started laughing and announced again to our friends that Bill's pants now had air conditioning.

Well, Bill got very quiet and I knew I had just made a mistake. I didn't really understand because his pants were torn and it was pretty obvious. If it had happened to me, I would have made fun of myself, but apparently that is not how men work.

When we got in the car, Bill asked, "Why did you make fun of me in front of them?"

"I didn't make fun of you," I replied.

"Yes, you did," he insisted.

"No, I didn't. I was just laughing with you."

"Oh, come on, Pam. You were laughing *at* me."

I probably shouldn't have, but I said, "Oh, brother. That is so immature."

At that, Bill stopped talking and wouldn't reengage in conversation until the next morning.

Driven to Succeed

What exactly is it about a man that makes his ego so reactive? As men, we have a built-in drive to succeed, which is the source of our fragile egos. A man's reactions come from the fact that he is adventurous. His particular pursuit is self-defined, so for some it is in the wilderness while for others it is in the office. Some men find their challenge in literature while others find it in athletics. Regardless of the pursuit, when life is easy, he is bored. When life is too challenging, he is discouraged. He is capable of remarkable feats of strength and courage. He is equally capable of astonishing feats of laziness and neglect.

Since we process life in boxes, we evaluate each thing in life separately. As I've mentioned, some of these boxes will be very attractive to some men because they know they can do the things in them well. Other boxes are unattractive because the men may not believe they can perform well there. If you are like me, you really want to spend time only in the boxes you are good at.

In these successful boxes, we want to be heroes. A man will put his heart and soul into the pursuits he has confidence in. He then wants his wife to make a big deal out of it. It is intoxicating when a woman says things like:

- You are so strong.
- You are so good at this.
- You are amazing.

In the same way, it is totally deflating when a woman says things like:

- That was stupid.
- I noticed, but what is the big deal?
- That took way too much time.

Unfortunately, this drive to succeed has a dark side. A man who realizes he is good at being lazy will fill his schedule with laziness. A man who constantly hears he is an underachiever will commit himself to underachieve for the rest of his life. If crudeness comes easily and is rewarded with laughter and attention, a man may just become an expert at being crude. If you are a man who had his confidence shaken early in life, you can develop a remarkable ability to disappoint people throughout your life.

Untamed Sophistication

In his insightful book *Wild at Heart*, John Eldredge captures the essence of what it means to be a man when he writes, "Adam, if you'll remember, was created outside the Garden, in the wilderness. . . . Man was born in the outback, from the untamed part of creation. . . . Adventure, with all its requisite danger and wildness, is a deeply spiritual longing written into the soul of man."[2]

Men want to conquer something, overcome something, discover something, kill something, or invent something. We are never interested in just keeping the status quo. God made us to subdue the earth and cultivate the ground. We are designed to face the wild things of life and bring them under submission. As a result, the last victory of a man's life is never enough to satisfy his soul. He will always need a new horizon to discover.

This is the way men learn in life. They venture out to the edge of what they are capable of, where they have to cry out to God for help. It is precisely at that point they learn to trust in God and they begin to walk by faith in the plans God has for their lives. This is how God has worked with men throughout the Bible. Consider the story of Abram in Genesis 12:1: "The LORD had said to Abram, 'Leave your country, your people and your father's household and go to the land I will show you.'"

Can you imagine Abram explaining the plan to Sarah? "Hey, Sarah, God told me today that we are going to move." What do you think Sarah's first question would have been? "Where are we moving, Abram?"

"I don't know, honey, but God will show us as we go."

"When do we leave?"

"Right away!"

God called Abram to pack up his entire family, as well as his business, and move to some unnamed country. Along the way, God would show him when the time was right. In order to follow God, Abram had to convince his wife and all the people for whom he was responsible that walking by faith was the best course of action.

Consider the feeding of the five thousand in Matthew 14. The disciples had become aware that the crowds have not eaten all day. They encouraged Jesus to send the people away so they could find food. In response, Jesus looked them squarely in the eyes and said, "You give them something to eat" (v. 16).

They must have been instantly overwhelmed, because they said, "We have here only five loaves of bread and two fishes" (v. 17). All they had was the equivalent of two lunches. The disciples humbly brought everything they had to Jesus; Jesus then put together their small resources with his huge resources so that those two lunches fed five thousand men plus their families.

In both of these cases, notice that Jesus initiated the action that took these men to the end of their resources. When they responded in faith, God did the unimaginable in their lives and every generation since has been talking about it.

The Winning Edge

The pursuit of adventure manifests itself often in a competitive nature. Men feel like warriors, so they are willing to turn anything into a game. We like to win at work and we like to win at play. We like to win at romance and we like to win at decision making. When we are not the winners, we must recover. We have great respect for those who beat us in any competitive pursuit, but we are always looking ahead to the next time when we can end up in the winner's circle.

Men, if, like me, you love sports, your testosterone shoots off the chart when your favorite team is winning. Likewise, when your team loses your testosterone level crashes.[3] The only conclusion you can reach is that you feel more like a man when you win!

Even when it comes to conversation we have an aggressive approach. We like to know where the conversation is going at all times. It is not that we want to control the conversation as much as we want to succeed at the conversation. As soon as we recognize something we can talk intelligently about, we want to jump in before the subject changes. We are easily intimidated by the women in our lives who can talk about anything at any time. We are amazed at men who can stay active in conversation. We are even highly critical of them because we don't want the pressure on us to have to be like them.

Guys Who Love Movies

When it comes time to choose a movie to watch, the battle between the sexes lights up. Men are exhilarated by watching a movie that is filled with dangerous scenes and outrageous adventures. The man who wins the woman's heart, while defeating the enemy with death-defying stunts, is the ultimate man because he knows no limits to success or his abilities. We love the hero. James Bond, Superman, Spider Man, and Ethan Hunt encompass all that we find exciting.

Most women wish we were more interested in stories of relationships and movies where real-life drama meets character development. But the question we all ask is, "Where is the danger? Where is the adventure? Where is the impossible situation that will be overcome by the hero of the day?" All of us men wonder, *Why would we want to be entertained by everyday matters when they are kind of confusing in real life?*

In *Star Trek: Generations*, Captain James T. Kirk meets up with Captain Jean-Luc Picard. They will explore together, conquer together, and reaffirm themselves as winners against the forces of evil and mediocrity. In a classic interchange that sums up everything it means to be a man, Captain Kirk says, "I take it the odds are against us and the situation is grim."

Captain Jean-Luc Picard responds, "You could say that."

Kirk says, "Sounds like fun!"

The Fantasy Avenger

The other side of the story is just sheer fantasy. We love to entertain thoughts of the impossible. We love to laugh at men in movies who overstate their worth and value. We love to stand with men who overshadow the reality of life. We know it is not realistic, but something about it transports us to a place in life that is better, more enjoyable, than the stable reality of today. It is not that we want to live in the fantasy of the greatness of the unconquerable male. We just want to visit there often enough to relieve the stress of real life.

In *Jurassic Park*, Ian Malcolm muses, "God creates dinosaurs. God destroys dinosaurs. God creates man. Man destroys God. Man creates dinosaurs—"

Dr. Ellie Sattler: "Dinosaurs eat man. Woman inherits the earth."

Ahh, the female gender keeps working its way into our delusions of grandeur. We like having women around, but we don't want them spoiling the dream. Man is a warrior and he wants a woman in his life who will pray for him as he goes out to battle and hug him when he returns from conquering evil. When she invades his world and tries to redefine it, he gets confused and frustrated.

What's a Man to Do?

Harnessing your ego is one of the most important steps of growth you can take as a man. How can you do this? Here are some steps.

Seek God's Adventure for Your Life

A man who is aimless or bored is overly reactive to his wife's opinions. Everything she says affects the emotional climate of his life. A man who is in partnership with God to accomplish something bigger than himself will be much more settled and less susceptible.

Laugh at Yourself

All of us do some really dumb things. There is no way to deny it, so you might as well enjoy it. As I mentioned in our book *Every Marriage Is a Fixer-Upper*, I have had some pretty funny moments in the weddings I have performed in my ministry. The worst thing I ever did was perform a wedding with my zipper down. I was wearing a wireless microphone that had an antenna that ran down my pant leg. I went to the bathroom to put this microphone on but forgot the last little detail!

Before entering the chapel at the next wedding I performed, I turned to the groomsmen and said, "Men, check your flies." I was wearing two microphones that day. The one that fed the house system was turned off but the one that fed the video camera was turned on. "Men, check your flies" is now permanently preserved right in the middle of the candle-lighting segment of the video.

Apologize Quickly

There is no way to retire your ego, so you are sometimes going to be offended or hurt or surprised. You can minimize the impact of these moments if you decide to take ownership of your reaction and say, "I'm sorry" to your wife.

What's a Woman to Do?

I (Pam) have learned that there are a few things a wife can do to help minimize the attacks on her husband's ego.

Compliment Often

Men are wired to respond to the encouragement of their wives. God has equipped each wife in such a way that she makes her husband's life better just by being around. When she decides to compliment her husband, her influence grows exponentially. Therefore, anytime you help your husband succeed in the adventure God has put on his heart, he falls in love with you.

Avoid All Public Criticism

Men get embarrassed easily and they hang on your words. As a result, it is a major violation anytime you criticize your husband in front of his friends or colleagues.

Stick to Decisions

Since we ladies can connect all of our lives together, we have a habit of continually processing information. Conversations with us can be confusing.

Just recently a friend of Bill's called his wife and said, "My brother has two free tickets for a round of golf this Saturday. What do you think?"

She said with excitement in her voice, "They are free? I think you should take advantage of that and play golf with your brother."

Well, to my friend, this sounded like a decision. He called his brother and committed to join him on the greens. He rose on Saturday before his wife woke up and headed for the golf course. Before he teed off at the first hole, he called his wife just to check in.

"Hi, honey. How are you doing?"

"Where are you?" she asked, a little irritated.

"I am golfing with my brother. We are about to tee off. Are you mad?"

"I can't believe you are going to leave me all alone to take care of our daughter again."

"We talked about this and you said it was okay."

"All I know is it is always about you. Enjoy your game, and I will enjoy my boring day."

With that, she hung up the phone as my friend fought back his anger.

This is brutal on a man because he wants to be a hero to his wife. If a woman changes her mind midstream, he doesn't know what the decision is, there is no way to succeed, and he has to retire his hero uniform to the closet.

 Each of you select one thing you can do that better handles a man's ego/sense of adventure.

• • •

A man, at his best, is refined and wild at the same time. He can be professional and polished while dreaming of the rugged outdoors. He can maintain a responsible life but he will never be captivated by it. His heart will always yearn for something bigger than life, even though he must master the rigors of his daily existence. The boxes on a man's waffle that are filled with adventure and wonder are inconvenient and disconcerting to those who love him the most, but they are what make him a man because they focus his heart.

A woman is an amazing creation: able to handle and focus on many things at one time, full of feeling, someone who loves to nurture others. We've also seen that there are times each month when many women, despite their best efforts, get stressed and reactionary and may seem downright mean. Husbands should keep in mind that their wives are battling physical symptoms they may harness but can't control and remember that the very thing they love about their wives—their femininity—is both wonderful and frustrating.

Husbands and wives, have mercy on each other!

The GIFT

Each of you make a "first-aid kit": she for his need for adventure (add in symbols and activities that build his sense of adventure so he doesn't feel such a need to protect his ego). You might want to include gifts of adventure: tokens for the batting cages, a new cool tool for the garage, or some trendy new electronic gizmo for him to figure out and install that will make him feel successful! He can make a first-aid kit for those PMS weeks that shows some TLC: chocolate, pampering equipment, a day at the spa, or his giving her a massage.

Go on a date and trade gifts.

 Unwrapping the GIFT

After adventure, a man can have sore muscles—and every month, a woman feels as if she has been hit by a truck or has the flu due to PMS. Select a relaxing activity you can do together. Take a long, warm bath together. Take turns giving a full body massage. While doing these things, talk about what other things bring a sense of rest, relaxation, or rejuvenation.

4

Capture Your Husband's Interest/ Connect to Your Wife's Heart

You are married today because you like the way you interrupt each other's lives. We've yet to meet the single who said, "What I really want is to load up on responsibility, get a big mortgage, and be totally overcommitted with someone." No, we think most people marry because when their mates entered their lives, it was like a knock on the door—a wonderful interruption that they wanted to go on and on romantically.

When you were dating, you were captivated with each other. Her smile, the way she walked, and her alluring personality captured your heart and redirected your attention. Every time your paths crossed or she called your name, you turned. You fell in love with her because she grabbed your attention like no one else you had ever met.

His smile, his eyes, and his interest in you connected the two of you and filled your heart with dreams of an incredible future together. You felt more complete around him, and you planned your days around the time you could spend with him. You fell in love with him because he convinced you he would value you forever.

Lurking around your love for one another, however, are two very cruel companions. They fancy themselves as bodyguards who protect you from unwanted pain and disappointment. Without being called, they show up in your relationship ready to rescue you from danger, both real and perceived. The problem with these two companions is that they are trying to protect you from a meaningful connection.

These two companions are *control* and *selfishness*. Because of the fall of mankind, women tend to be controllers and men tend to be selfish.

Before we get very far in the conversation, we do want to say that generally, men and women are sincerely motivated. Women control because they have a desire to make things better. Men selfishly assert their way because they want to be successful and are afraid to change once they have discovered a way that works.

Let's take a look at these tendencies.

Women Feel a Need to Control

A woman can sense when things are not as good as they could be. Her thoughts and emotions are stirred and her energy level begins to climb. She instantly develops an opinion about what could be done to improve the situation. Once she has an opinion, she feels responsible for the people involved and, hence, the opinions get stronger. At this point, she has to say and/or do something.

If her husband heeds her advice and the situation gets better, things calm down and her sense of value goes up. If, on the other hand, he ignores her advice or the situation gets worse, she feels an even greater sense of responsibility. She will put more effort into it. She may make a frontal attack and hit the "problem" head-on until it is resolved or she may come back to it over and over again, until she has worn down the people involved and won them over to her point of view.

We mistakenly think that women have to be right all the time. You have probably heard the comical quote, "I was thrilled when I found Mrs. Right. I just didn't know her first name was Always." The reality is that she doesn't need to be right all the time, she just needs to make things better. A woman will often make fun of herself and point out her mistakes. She doesn't mind accepting her flaws and recognizing her shortcomings as long as this makes the situation better than it was before. She also doesn't mind pointing out her husband's flaws and shortcomings if she believes it will make the situation better.

Control Gone Amuk

One time Bill had the opportunity to advance his career by attending a three-day pastors' conference in the Portland, Oregon, area. I wanted to make the trip better for him so I told him I would go too. I had talked to my mom and she was willing to take care of our son, Brock.

We dropped our son off at Grandma's and drove twelve hours to get to the conference. We spent Thursday, Friday, and Saturday intensely learning about ministry and networking with colleagues. By the end of the conference, we were tired but excited about the new things we had learned. Satisfied that I had made Bill's life better, it was time to get back to my mom's house to rescue her from our son and make *her* life better!

"Pam, this has been an awesome few days and we have a big trip in front of us. I think we should drive to the edge of Portland, get a hotel, and then get up early in the morning to drive to your mom's house."

The voice sounded similar to my husband's but I knew it couldn't possibly be his because my mom was anxiously waiting for us to rush home and improve her existence.

"I'll finish packing my suitcase while you start loading the car," I said, ignoring the ridiculous suggestion Bill had made.

"Pam, did you hear what I said? I think we should spend the night in Portland and leave early in the morning."

He said it again! I couldn't believe it. Didn't he understand that my mom's life would be ruined if we didn't drive all night so we could get to her house first thing in the morning? He obviously wasn't thinking about Brock either. It is traumatic for a preschooler to be away from his mom for more than four days. Grandma is good, but only Mom can make things all right!

"We can't do that!" I blurted out. "We need to get to Idaho by morning and you love to drive at night. That way we can spend all day Sunday with Mom before we leave for home. It will be better that way."

"I don't know, Pam. I really think it would be better—"

"It wouldn't be better for me. We need to leave tonight." I knew this would leverage the discussion, get us on the road, and give Bill time to adjust his perspective.

So, off we went on our trek across the Oregon desert late at night. Well, I underestimated just how tired we both were. At about ten o'clock, Bill asked if I would drive for a while because he was getting too sleepy to stay awake. I was determined to make things better so, of course, I took over the wheel. By midnight, I was too tired to continue also, so I woke Bill up and asked him to take over driving. He agreed because he could tell I was still intent on my plan.

By one o'clock it was evident that we were not going to make it to Idaho, but we were in the middle of nowhere. There was nothing on the horizon except a whole lot of sand, a collection of unfriendly cactus, and a landscape of dry brush.

Bill told me I would have to drive the rest of the way if we were going to drive straight through. I had to humbly admit that I didn't have it in me either, so I reluctantly agreed that we would stop at the next hotel we found. Thirty minutes later we arrived at the Oregon border and encountered our only option. It was a motel designed for truckers and vagabonds. I think the name of the motel was the Dare to Stay. It was strategically located right next to the train tracks.

The guy behind the counter was missing more teeth than he possessed and was working a big wad of chew in his lower lip. He spit out the tobacco juice and asked us, "Do you want the room by the day or by the hour?" We were too embarrassed to say we just wanted it for a few hours so we paid for a whole day.

The key was stamped *Room 103*. We are still not sure why he gave us a key because the lock on the door did not work! In our exhaustion, we pushed the door open and were assaulted by the décor. The walls were covered with red velour wallpaper. A life-size portrait of Elvis hung at the head of the bed. The bedspread was horribly stained and there was a worn trail in the red shag carpet from the bed to the bathroom. Just to make things interesting, a coin-operated Magic Fingers box on the nightstand offered to vibrate the bed and add a little extra "pleasure" to our stay.

This was definitely not "better," but I figured I could improve things just enough to get us some sleep. I sent Bill to the car to fish out the beach towels. I laid them on the bed so we would not have to come in contact with the disgusting linens. We moved the dresser in front of the door to act as a lock. We would sleep completely dressed, just in case we slipped off the beach towels.

Having satisfied myself that the situation was as good as it was going to get, we laid down to get some much needed rest. As we drifted off into sweet slumber, a train shook the building as it announced its arrival with a horn blast that would have wakened the dead. I am not sure, but I think the train whistle was tuned to say, "Don't even think about getting any sleep. My friends and I will be coming by all night to check in on you. I dare you to sleep at the Dare to Stay motel. Ha, ha, ha." From that point on, a train came by every hour, on the hour, to announce our foolishness.

After five one-hour naps, we climbed out of bed, moved the dresser, threw the beach towels in the trunk, and said "Good-bye" to the King. Since our trackside resort failed to make things better, I set my sights on the rest of the trip and told myself, *I am pretty sure nothing else on this trip will be quite as bad as spending the night with a velvet Elvis.*

As you can see, my controlling nature set us up for a lot of frustration that trip.

Men Feel a Need to Be Selfish

A man loves it when he discovers an area of life in which he can succeed. He goes to work with a sense of pride and the anticipation that he will provide for his family well. He chooses hobbies that fit his skill set. He looks for ways to get his wife interested in sex and believes their relationship is always improved by sexual activity. He assumes she feels the same way, even though she is resistant to the idea that all they need to do is have sex and life will look better.

He is afraid to let his wife make too many decisions because she might make things so complicated that he can no longer succeed in his life. At the same time, he is hesitant to make decisions himself because she voluntarily evaluates them. Her reaction triggers his sense of inadequacy and makes him feel as if he doesn't know what he is doing.

As a result, a man tends to be selfish. He wants the family to organize around his schedule and make his career the priority. He wants to have free time when he wants free time. He wants his wife to take care of whatever chores he does not want to be bothered with and he wants her to do it without complaining. He wants her always to look good and to be forever fascinated with him. He wants her to listen to him and take his advice on anything he feels smart about. The things in life that confuse him, however, he wants her to just figure out. In a word, a man wants his life to be simple enough that he can feel successful and he wants his wife to make it this way.

Selfishness Gone Amuk

It was our second year of marriage and I decided to do it up big for Pam's birthday. I set out to do everything I knew she loved. We started in the afternoon with swimming because I know she loves the water. I then took her to the mall and gave her exactly thirty minutes to locate and buy the perfect dress. Then I pulled her out of the dress shop and dragged her immediately to the deli stand to get crackers and cheese, because I know she loves cheese. I rushed her to the salon for a foot massage and pedicure because I know she loves those and I paced because the pedicurist seemed slower than molasses. The procedure ended just in time for us to make it to a romantic movie, because I know she loves romance. As soon as the movie was over, I told her we needed to try to be the first ones out of the theater. I was taking her to a surprise party because I know she loves surprises.

At that point, Pam was more than a little frustrated. I thought she would appreciate what I was doing but she was feeling very rushed. She said, "What I really wanted was time together. What I feel I am getting is deadlines. Do we really have to do all of this in such a hurry?"

I got kind of mad. I was trying to be her hero and I wanted her to be incredibly proud of me by the end of the night. I had rationalized that I was doing all this for her. In reality, I was doing it for the reaction I would *get from* her. Since she wasn't reacting the way I wanted her to, I was upset. I realized, after the fact, that I was making her birthday about me. I was more concerned about how she felt about me than how she felt.

This selfishness manifests itself along two extremes. At times, a man will demand his wife do what he wants. He will demand they have sex, demand she spend money differently, demand she make more time for him, demand she serve him and meet his needs. At other times, he will engage in avoidance. He will avoid conversation, involvement with the family, the list of tasks that he needs to complete, and issues that he needs to confront. All the while, he cannot understand why his wife gets so frustrated with him because, in his mind, he is making a great contribution to the family.

Cute or Controlling?

The upside is that we have remarkable influence on one another. When you are good to one another, life gets better. You have a way of triggering good thoughts and good feelings in one another. At the same time, you are capable of triggering the negative messages you believe about yourselves. There are certain things a woman does that make her husband think she is cute. When he feels this way about her, he is attracted to her, attentive to her, and thrilled to have her in his life.

There are other things a woman does that makes her husband think she is controlling. When he feels this way about her, he distances himself from her, is reminded of his own inadequacies, and develops an intense desire to run away from whatever situation is causing the pain.

It is cute when you as a wife:	It is controlling when you as a wife:
Flirt with your husband. This is one of the things that attracted him to you in the first place. A light touch, an intriguing stare, a soft voice all communicate that he is attractive, heroic, and capable.	Use seductive looks, tone of voice, and teasing to get your husband to do chores for you. He is painfully aware of his vulnerability in this area. When you dress provocatively, talk seductively, and offer yourself sexually, he will say yes to anything you ask. When you resort to this, however, he feels used afterwards and despises the fact that he is such an easy mark.
Laugh at your husband's jokes. Your laughter is intoxicating. It makes your husband feel smart, witty, and strong. He longs to be around you when you make him feel good about his sense of humor.	Make fun of your husband in public. As we mentioned in the last chapter, he hates to admit it, but his ego is fragile. He wants you to be proud of him and brag about him to both your friends and his friends. When he points out his flaws in public, he is being vulnerable. Since he chose to do it, he is not hurt by it. When you point out his flaws in public, however, he feels like a failure. Since he lives with the illusion that you think everything about him is awesome, it blindsides him and knocks him off balance.
Make your husband's life easier by making dinner, cleaning house, or handling a task that is stressful to him. This is not to say that these tasks are "women's work." The issue is that	Complain about responsibilities you have agreed to take charge of. Men like agreements. They put life in neat boxes so they know what to do and what not to do. As soon as you agree

It is cute when you as a wife:	It is controlling when you as a wife:
he likes life to be simple enough to realize success. Anything you do that makes success attainable will draw him to you. He may like to cook but finds gardening stressful. He may love to do yard work but finds bill paying nerve-racking. If you take on the task he finds strenuous, you get better-looking to him.	to take charge of some area, he can relax about it and take it off his plate. When you complain about it, he gets confused and wonders why you ever talked about it in the first place. He feels forced to deal with something he agreed to let go. This complicates his life and makes him feel as if the relationship is not working.
Listen to your husband. Men have a hard time talking with people at an emotional level. Few men have the kind of friends that share fears, dreams, heartaches, and the heroic notions they have about themselves. When your husband married you, he was hoping he would have the opportunity to share these things with you. Since he has little or no practice with this skill, his feelings are fragile and easily bruised. When you patiently listen without judgment, he discovers an experience in life he has with no one else.	Hijack the conversation and steer it in the direction you want it to go. You are probably better at conversation than your husband and you get excited when he wants to talk. You assume he converses the same way you do, so you fully engage when he begins. It isn't long before you are sharing your thoughts and concerns and you mistakenly believe they are welcome. Instead, your husband concludes he is not very good at this and might as well not share because you will take over the conversation anyway. As a result, he stops listening to you and you fail to discover what is really going on with him.
Reach an agreement with your husband. It doesn't matter whether the issue is finances, scheduling, the kids' activities, or home responsibilities: anytime your husband senses you are on the same page with him, he feels good about himself. He knows	Act as if a decision that was made between the two of you was just a conversation. This happens because you are constantly processing life. Every conversation can change everything for you. You have been doing this your whole life, so it doesn't

It is cute when you as a wife:	**It is controlling when you as a wife:**
how to proceed and he becomes convinced that life is going to work with you. His stress level drops and his confidence grows.	seem like a big deal to you. Your husband, on the other hand, has been simplifying things his whole life. He likes the bottom line and wants to know how to succeed in your marriage and in the workplace. When a decision has been made, he begins to take action. When he discovers later that it wasn't a decision, he feels he wasted his time and he grows passive in the relationship.
Let your husband brag about his accomplishments. All of us men are fascinated by what we do. We want to stop to relive the golf game, the project we built, the move we discovered on the video game, the new muscles we built at the gym, the wisdom we discovered in the Bible or at work, and so on. We know, deep down, that it is silly but we love it nonetheless. When you encourage us to tell you about our exploits, we fall in love again and again.	Criticize your husband's career choice or hobbies. A man's career and hobbies are reflections of who he is. They are not just activities they engage in to provide for the family. In fact, a man who works simply to pay bills will become either bored or angry over time. As a result, there is a restlessness in your husband until he finds the career and hobbies that allow him to be who he really is. When you criticize his choices, you criticize him and give him the message, "You are deficient and you should change."
Help your husband succeed in his career. Since your husband's work is a reflection of who he believes he is, anything you do to help him makes him feel more confident and worthwhile. It may be hands-on help, such as bookkeeping or office work, or it	Make commitments for your husband without asking him. As he pursues his career, he makes commitments and focuses himself on conquering the challenge at hand. When you surprise him with obligations you have added, he is forced to redefine

It is cute when you as a wife:	It is controlling when you as a wife:
may be providing time for him to do what is necessary to succeed. Either way, he thinks you are awesome when you make his career easier to pursue.	his schedule and his strategy for success. If this happens too many times, he will begin to conclude there is no use making plans because you will change them all. Against his best intentions, he will begin to pull away and become passive in the relationship.
Create a vibrant emotional atmosphere in your home. God has given you the ability to set the atmosphere in your home. When you are happy, everyone is happy. When you are upset, everyone is upset. When you are scared, everyone is off balance. This is a tall order, but when you greet your husband with enthusiasm and choose joy as your response to life, your husband finds you very attractive.	Use emotions to manipulate your husband. The average man is not nearly as emotionally skilled as you are. You have been interacting with your emotions your whole life and have developed a high degree of skill in expressing them and utilizing them to make your life more effective. Your husband, on the other hand, is a newcomer to this game and feels overmatched. When you use emotions to get what you want, he will eventually feel you have conned him and will likely resent your superior ability to get your way.
Encourage your husband to pursue male solutions to his issues. Men are wired to conquer something, fix something, or figure something out. When he does this, he feels better about himself and his confidence grows. He is easier to live with and will make better decisions in the future.	Give female answers to male issues. You love your husband and you want to do all you can to make his life better. As a result, you get very interested in his conversations and want to give him advice that helps him see life more clearly. The problem comes when you give him advice that ignores his aggressive nature or ties too many issues together.

It is cute when you as a wife:	It is controlling when you as a wife:
Encourage your husband to pursue the adventure God has put in his heart. God builds strength in his life by leading him into situations that take him to the edge of his abilities. At this point, he needs to call out to God for help. Then he discovers a walk of faith that energizes his life and expands his horizons.	Push your husband to play it safe. Discretion in a man is a virtue, but a man who is tame and plays it safe all the time has put aside the dream God put in his heart. He will either shut down his heart or grow angry. He may no longer cause you any trouble, but he will not fascinate you or carry the burdens of life with you.
Ask your husband what he plans to do. Your husband is looking for ways to succeed. When you encourage him to make decisions, he grows in confidence and ventures forward in his leadership. When you discourage his decision making, he concludes you do not respect him and will react in a negative way.	Tell your husband what to do. Your interest in your husband's life gives you great insight. As a result, you often feel the need to comment on his actions and decisions. This is great when he asks for your advice, but when you boldly tell him what he ought to be doing, he loses self-confidence. When you offer unnecessary opinions, you send a message that he is less than competent.

Sexy or Selfish?

In the same way, there are certain things you can do as a husband that will make your wife think you are sexy and attractive. As you do these things, her interest in you grows emotionally, physically, and socially. There are, however, other things that you can say or do as a husband that send a message of selfishness. These messages trigger off in her the belief that she is not worth very much to you. She will then react in some way. She may get irritable or she may become insecure. She may grow quiet and cold or she may become combative and intense. She will present you with a series of tests to see just how important she is.

It is as if God has built in an early warning system for a man's tendency toward selfishness. When he is sacrificing for his wife, she is more content and simple to live with. When he is being selfish, she becomes more complicated and difficult to live with.

It is sexy when you as a husband:	It is selfish when you as a husband:
Listen to your wife. She is wired to connect her heart to yours. She wants to share as much of her life with you as possible. When you listen to her with interest, her heart draws close to you, you get better-looking to her, and all your words sound wiser to her.	Fix your wife's problems while she is emotionally connecting with you. God made her to connect her whole life together emotionally. As soon as things are connected, problem solving is evident to her. When you interrupt the connection process by trying to solve her problems for her, you disrupt the way God has made her and frustrate her.
Come to your wife's rescue. Anytime she is overwhelmed with life and you step in to help her, she falls in love with you. It may be help with her car, with money, or with a decision over a circumstance that has taken an unexpected turn.	Call your wife "stupid." Since she carries the burden for her whole life with her all the time, it is not uncommon for her to overcommit herself or to make quick decisions that require "fixing" after the fact. When you respond to these moments with comments such as, "Can't you ever get it right?" or "What were you thinking?" you crush her spirit and create distance in your relationship.
Provide opportunities for your wife to grow. She has a reservoir of hopes and dreams in her heart. She will share them with you early on in your	Complain about steps of growth your wife attempts to take. You love having your wife around. Life is just easier when she plans her schedule

It is sexy when you as a husband:

It is selfish when you as a husband:

marriage because she feels she can trust you with them. If you commit yourself to make these dreams a reality, she becomes your greatest fan and will reward you with encouragement, cooperation, and a fun sex life. Ephesians 5:25–27 says to "love your wives, just as Christ loved the church and gave himself up for her . . . to present her to himself as a radiant church, without stain or wrinkle or any other blemish, but holy and blameless." You are at your best as a husband when you help your wife be her best.

around yours and keeps herself available to you. If she is going to grow to become all she can be, she needs time. When you encourage her to grow but then complain about the time it takes, you confuse her and direct her heart away from you.

Sacrifice for your wife. Just as you are wired for success, she is wired to feel valued. Anytime you give her the message "You are worth it," you touch the deepest part of her. The message of value raises her energy level, softens her heart, and boosts her confidence. No matter what it is, if it was a sacrifice on your part, she will feel more valuable to you.

Make your wife feel guilty for all the work you "have to do for her." When you blame her for "making you do it," she will feel devalued and will resent the help you have given. Since there are some things in life she cannot physically do, this puts her in a bind. She needs you to lift heavy things and handle tasks she does not understand, but asking you to do these things will make her feel worse about herself.

Get to know your wife. Since she loves to be valued, the time you spend getting to know her physically, emotionally, spiritually, and socially adds to her sense of worth. It is interesting that the Bible refers to sexual

Ignore your wife. You will find that other tasks are simpler than trying to understand your wife. The TV, the garage, the computer, yard work, and golf are all much easier pursuits than developing intimacy with the lady of

It is sexy when you as a husband:	**It is selfish when you as a husband:**
intimacy this way: "Adam *knew* Eve his wife, and she conceived" (Gen. 4:1 NKJV, emphasis added).	your dreams. Over time, it is easy to fall into the trap of ignoring your wife to get other things done. This will make your wife think that everything else in life is more important than her. She will most likely create conflict in order to get your attention. It is easy to misinterpret the conflict as a message that she doesn't like you so you avoid her even more. This leads to more conflict and so on. It is, in the long run, much easier to spend time with her on a regular basis and stay curious about who she is becoming.
Remember important details in your wife's life. Certain memories have a very special place in your wife's heart. For sure, her birthday and your anniversary are vital. The dates you celebrate may also include the first time you kissed, the day you proposed, the death of a loved one, the date of her baptism, and so on. It is wise for you to find out what these dates are and write them on your calendar. As you remember them, year after year, she will get the message that you value her for who she is.	Treat your wife as if she is invisible. As you begin your career, you will meet many interesting people. You will make decisions with them and quote them when you come home. If you do this but fail to make decisions with your wife and remain fascinated by her, she will begin to feel she doesn't matter. She will conclude that you notice everyone else in the world but have stopped noticing her. This is never good!
Help out with responsibilities. Your wife has a list of what is important to her. It may include keeping the house in order, keeping the cars clean, putting every activity on a	Make comments about some tasks in life being "women's work." Your wife views your life as a joint venture. She assumes you care about her life and everything that goes along with being

It is sexy when you as a husband:	It is selfish when you as a husband:
family calendar, or being involved at your church.	connected to her. Therefore, everything she is responsible for, she wants you to notice. When she needs help, she wants you to jump in. When something needs to be done and she has run out of time to complete it, she wants you to throw your hat in the ring and tackle the task at hand.
View the tasks, activities, and concerns of your wife's life as "our concerns." She has dreamed of having a soul mate in life. She longs for you to be the one who shares all of life—the dreams, the hopes, the heartaches, the pain, and the glory. When she is upset, she wants you to be upset (but not out of control). When she is happy, she wants you to be happy. When she is concerned about some issue in the family or the community, she wants you to share the same sense of alarm over the issue.	Tell your wife not to bother you with her "dumb stuff." To her, there is no "dumb stuff." Since everything is connected, everything is important. When you tell her not to worry, to allow others to deal with it, or to just let it go, you are asking her to not be a woman.
Provide acceptance so that your wife can be herself. Your wife is fun, fretful, responsible, spontaneous, complicated, straightforward, coy, seductive, and self-conscious all at the same time. She faces some days in life with incredible courage and boldness. She faces other days with trepidation and fear. She is kind and gentle but can become fierce and defensive at a moment's notice. She	Expect your wife to respond to life the way you do. Men like the results of estrogen because it makes their wives beautiful. However, they aren't too thrilled with the fallout. Every month, your wife will go through a cycle of ups and downs that will swing her moods, fluctuate her self-worth, and challenge her kindness. When you expect her to act like you, you create an impossible situation

It is sexy when you as a husband:	It is selfish when you as a husband:
doesn't like the changing landscape of her life any more than you do but she must live with it. When you give her freedom to be this ever-changing individual, her life calms down and her heart warms up.	for her. As soon as she realizes you do not accept her as a woman, she will grow defensive and express her displeasure to you consistently.

STOP Did you see yourself in any of the "selfish" or "controlling" boxes? Don't point them out in each other—that will just cause a fight and hurt feelings. Instead, own your issues and shortcomings, and each of you select one area in which you want to trade control for cute or selfish for sexy. Share your desire to change with your mate and then each of you respond to your mate's desire to change with "Wow, thanks! I really appreciate your honesty. I want you to know that I don't expect overnight change. It is a gift to me just to know you recognize you want to work to safeguard our love."

This kind of response to a spouse's self-disclosure will move your relationship forward much better than:

- Well, about time!

- Yeah, I know! And it is so annoying.

- So glad you finally figured it out!

- Duh!

A sarcastic or negative response shuts your spouse down. Some of the best advice we ever got was in one of our wedding cards, which simply said, "Take sarcasm out of your relationship."

Ten Surefire Ways to Wreck Love

As relationship specialists for over twenty-five years, we've seen it all. We have observed that there are ten very common mistakes couples make in the first five years that will really mess up love. Really, when a relationship dissolves, it boils down to one of two things: someone was selfish, or someone did something really stupid.

So if you really want to mess up your future, do one of these selfish and stupid things:

1. Call up an old boyfriend or girlfriend and hang out.
2. Compare your mate to your ex.
3. Get involved in pornography, go to a strip club, or call a 900 number "love" line.
4. Run up your credit card bills.
5. Give into a drug, alcohol, gambling, or shopping addiction.
6. Sit on the sofa instead of getting a job.
7. Scream at, belittle, or hit your spouse.
8. Lie.
9. Run home to mom and dad every time there is an argument.
10. Actually believe that "What happens in Vegas, stays in Vegas."

Two Simple Steps to Success in Marriage

There are many ways to mess up love because we humans have a bent toward selfish, controlling, and basically stupid choices. However, God helped us out. To have a supersuccessful relationship, there are really two basic steps, two simple ingredients:

1. Be near God.
2. Be nice.

If you, as an individual, stay close to God and "abide in Christ," meaning that every moment of every day your heart says, "God, I want to do life your way," then God becomes your personal marriage coach. His Spirit will whisper, "Let's try saying what you just said in a better way." "Say you're sorry." "Do something romantic tonight." Undercover and Secret Service agents wear microphones hidden in their ears so they can protect people like the president. God is like that microphone when it comes to protecting your love. He will whisper what to do (or not do) to you. If you obey, you can win at love.

And the second, "Be nice," should be so obvious that you do it by nature. Unfortunately, it is not natural to be nice so we end up being hardest on the people we love the most! In reality, it takes so little to be nice. If you open doors, put away the dishes, pick up the house, bring him a glass of water, your spouse is drawn to you. It is the little things that will add up to create a loving environment in your new home.

It is a little like the math formula: $1 + 1 = 2$. So "be near God" + "be nice" = a beautiful sex life. It is really quite simple, even though we complicate it with emotional reactions and poor choices. Do things God's way and God will bless.

Picture God's perfect plan as the two of you standing under an umbrella in the rain. The umbrella is God's hand of goodness, anointing, love, and favor. Love thrives when the two of you are together under God's protection. On the other hand, love gets strenuous when one of you moves out from under the umbrella. The spouse who moved shouldn't drag the other into the rain. Instead, he or she should get back under the umbrella and covering provided when you walk under God's plan for marriage.

To do this, you will want to daily, moment by moment, say no to your own fleshly lusts and say yes to the Spirit. If you both do this, your love stays centered under God's umbrella of favor. A good place to be!

STOP Take a moment here to practice getting under God's umbrella of shelter for your love. Together pray and say something like, "God, since you created love and marriage, we want to run our relationship your way."

Iron Sharpens Iron

The big problem with control and selfishness is that they actually encourage your spouse to be immature. A man who needs to be controlled is just a child in an adult body. A woman who needs to control has not learned to build mature trust in her relationship with either God or her husband. A man who responds to his wife with selfish tactics exposes his belief that she is too immature to consult on the areas of life that are important to him. A man who consistently plans his life around his selfish desires has not developed the maturity to be a servant to either his Savior or his wife.

Instead of selfishness and control, decide you'd rather be selfless and trusting. God encourages us to be "iron sharpening iron," meaning we are better people after spending time with each other (see Proverbs 27:17). This isn't always easy. Being the firstborn in my family, I (Pam) have a bent toward bossiness, so my first year of marriage I had to make myself practice saying, "I trust you, Bill." The first five years I thanked Bill for decisions he made for our new family, even if I didn't always completely agree with the method. I had to learn that just because Bill might do something differently than I would that doesn't mean he did it wrong. Lots of times decisions are just preferences.

In the same way, I (Bill) had to practice placing Pam's needs in front of my own, even if she seemed a bit high-maintenance at times! Pam struggled a lot in our early marriage with migraines, so my job was to lend aid, not complain she was raining on my parade. And because of emotional scars from her childhood, she sometimes overreacted when I hurt her feelings. I had to take many a deep breath and say, "Pam, tell me how you are feeling," when I wanted to yell, "Oh, come on! You've got to be kidding!" As time passed, we both got better at managing our tendencies toward control and selfishness. You will too.

• • •

It's raining out there in the world and God gave you each other for love and companionship—so buy an umbrella to remind the two of you to stay under the favor of God!

The GIFT

What phrase do you need to practice so you can help raise your spouse's confidence after spending time with you? Don't tell your spouse what the phrase is—just begin to use it!

Unwrapping the GIFT

The Bible gives some ideas on words that are better than the selfish or controlling ones:

- Let your speech always be with grace, as though seasoned with salt, so that you will know how you should respond to each person. (Colossians 4:6 NASB)

- But now you also, put them all aside: anger, wrath, malice, slander, and abusive speech from your mouth. (Colossians 3:8 NASB)

- Let no unwholesome word proceed from your mouth, but only such a word as is good for edification according to the need of the moment, so that it will give grace to those who hear. (Ephesians 4:29 NASB)

Bring these better words into the bedroom. Sit or stand facing each other and take turns undressing one another. As you do this, compliment body parts and your spouse's inner character. Let the words clothe you with new confidence and care.

Part Two

Invest in Great Sex

Everything Looks Better After Sex

5

Soulful, Satisfying Sex

Everything looks better after sex. You are in a fight, an argument over who is supposed to do what when—then you get turned on by the passion in her eyes, one thing leads to another, and you two discover yourselves in bed with a "who cares who did what or when" attitude. Something that seemed so important seems insignificant in light of the magnificent intimate time you just experienced.

Perhaps it's this scenario: you are worried over the mortgage/rent, your college tuition or school loan, the car payment—until you realize that sometimes all you do really need is love—and a bed—in a room with some privacy. Sex has a way of leveling the playing field. It dawns on you that people both rich and poor can have soulful, satisfying sex—as long as you are still rich enough to own your own bed and rent four walls to put around it!

Why is it that the issues of life can seem so essential to resolve except when you're in the throes of passion? Because sex is a gift, a gift from God to make all the hard work of maintaining a relationship, building a family, and being the cornerstone of the church and community worth it. Sex is God's payoff, God's reward system for responsible living—or at least that is what God designed it for.

Why Sex?

Let's see if we can provide an overview of just why God would create such an amazing gift.

Sex Is More Fun Than an Arcade!

This is the most obvious. Sex is outright pleasurable. The Bible story of Isaac and Rebekah presents sex as recreational. Isaac had been trying to pass Rebekah off as his sister to save his own neck, but the king spotted them "sporting" with each other (Gen. 26:8 KJV). The king was as mad as a hornet because it was obvious to him that Rebekah was definitely not Isaac's sister! They were having too much "fun" together. The point is obvious: sex is pleasurable because God made it that way!

Sex Is More Powerful Than Dynamite!

Sex is like the superglue that can hold a couple together through very rocky times. A couple we've known for over twenty years have experienced some really hard times together. When they were newlyweds, he was nearly killed in a work accident. They have teetered on the brink of financial ruin more than once. But they kept investing in their sex life. They are so cemented together that job loss, prodigal children, disease, career setbacks—nothing can shake this rock-solid couple.

Once the wife said to me (Pam), "I am so glad we had sex nearly every day in those early years because those memories now get us through tough things. It's like those first few years trained us. When stress comes now, we instinctively reach out for one other instead of reaching out to someone else."

Sex Is Like a Thermometer

You can read how your relationship is doing by your sex life. If you feel close and in rhythm with each other, sex happens almost effortlessly and often. If you are not getting along, the times between sexual encounters becomes longer and longer.

Sex Is Like a Thermostat

Sex isn't just an indicator of how you are doing—you can also "set" your sex life, just as you can flip the switch and turn on the air conditioning on a hot summer day. You can schedule sex! You can put light at the end of your responsibility tunnel and keep an environment of tender, loving care in your marriage by scheduling sex. Enjoy the times when sex is more spontaneous and combustible, but by scheduling sex, you can help keep the home fires of passion burning strong.

The number-one reason for us to schedule sex is that our schedules fill up easily and we can quickly find ourselves drifting apart simply because we didn't make sex a priority. We wrote our book *Red-Hot Monogamy* to give couples an eight-week incentive plan for moving their relationship to the front burner. So in our Outlook schedules on our computers and in our PDAs, we have the initials RHM (*Red-Hot Monogamy*) down as a weekly date night. When someone asks for an appointment, we look at our PDAs and simply reply, "Oh, I'm sorry, that night won't work. I have a prior engagement!"

Our RHM dates move time slots depending on our responsibilities. When teens entered the picture, the morning became much more appealing because we knew they were in school and wouldn't pop in with their friends! When the children were babies, once a week Bill hopped home for our own version of "nap time."

We actually have three separate times each week that make sex more likely:

1. Our weekly date night, which is four hours of private time. We can do anything we want with that time, and this often leads to sex.

2. Our weekly breakfast and workout time. We often start our day with sex—it motivates and energizes us for the rest of our day.

3. Scheduled sex time. We usually place this on a separate day and time from the date night.

Hopefully even in the worst of weeks, one or two of these opportunities for sex will actually work out! (And scheduling sex usually makes you more in the mood for spontaneous sex too!)

STOP Pull out those PDAs, your paper calendar, or datebook and create a time each week for sex. Get out your stylus or pen and make a date for sex—right now. Put a bookmark here so you'll know where to pick up our discussion once you are back—because we know sex can also be disorienting. It will be easy to forget where you left off and some really important stuff is still ahead in this chapter!

Sex Is Like a Manufacturing Plant

Sex is productive. The natural results of having sex is that you will produce heirs—children! The consequences of children are much happier when you are in a strong, stable marriage. This is the main reason God created sex for a marriage. Sex comes with responsibility. It is a joyous one, but it is also a long-term, constant responsibility. Psalm 127:3 says, "Behold, children are a gift of the LORD, / The fruit of the womb is a reward" (NASB). So this reinforces that God's gifts of love multiply into more gifts of love. Sex itself is a gift, and the results of sex are a gift.

Sex Is Better Than Bowflex

Sex is a great workout. Yes, sex burns calories. Sexual intercourse burns about 150 calories per half hour, which is about the same as walking 4.8 kilometers (or approximately three miles per hour).[1] It will be a while before you'll see it marketed as a diet plan, though, because the average sexual experience burns up about fifty calories. It would take a whole lot of sex to actually lose weight, but it is a whole lot more fun than a treadmill or a bike ride!

Sex Is Way Better Than Drugs!

Sex gives an emotional high. Sex releases endorphins. Sex resets your happiness clock. Life is stressful for everyone, so we all need ways to cope with the demands. Many turn to illegal drugs, alcohol, or extreme busyness. The most effective stress reliever, however, is to be in love with someone in a deeply committed relationship—Jesus first, then a human being! This type of relationship with Jesus leads to peace, confidence, and the ability to love someone else from the heart. This type of relationship with your spouse will result in satisfying sex that ignites your body and inspires your soul.

If you are feeling depressed, sex will help. The hard part is that you usually don't want to allow someone to get that close if you are blue. You aren't in the mood even though sex may be one of the very best mood lifters there is. Sex is a cardio workout, and it has skin touching skin in a pleasurable way. As a result, natural endorphins are released, your mood is elevated, pain is dissipated, and euphoria is instated!

Sex Is Better Than X-ray Vision

We've mentioned that the popular Old Testament term used to refer to sex is "to know." It is the ability to allow yourself to be so enraptured with your spouse that he or she feels completely safe and able to let his or her guard down. This is truly what makes sex so powerful and meaningful.

This is also what sex was created to be in the Garden of Eden, before the fall of man. Adam and Eve were "naked and were not ashamed" (Gen. 2:25 NASB). By its very nature, sex requires you to become naked physically, but great sex—soulful and satisfying sex—also allows your souls to be naked before one another. This kind of safe vulnerability can lead to breakthroughs into how your spouse is wired, what is really going on in his or her heart and mind. When the trust level is built up by one good sexual experience after another, not only are you willing to risk and try new things sexually, you become willing to risk emotionally as well. You gain the ability to trust your mate at the deepest levels.

Sex can be a safe place where life's strongest emotions can be expressed. That is why couples reach out across the darkness of the deepest sadness and find comfort in each other's arms when they have experienced great loss. And it is also why sex is so often the celebration after a raise, a promotion, or some groundbreaking news. We want to share all the best of life with our mates in a way that is unique to the marriage relationship.

Sex Is Like the Declaration of Interdependence

Just as the Declaration of Independence set a whole new plan in motion in the United States, every time you enjoy sex within the context of marriage, you announce God's plan of love for humankind. Your love is a lighthouse. The love you share is one of the most powerful ways that you two can declare your faith in God. It is a personal relationship with Jesus Christ that gives you the power to be a caring, compassionate life partner instead of a selfish, stupid creep. The fruit of the Spirit is love, joy, peace, patience, kindness, goodness, faithfulness, self-control—all the things that make a good marriage great! (Gal. 5:22–23). These are the traits that make for a sizzling sex life. So when you love each other with God's power, people notice.

We went to Bible college and seminary. We have all kinds of biblical facts in our minds. We have memorized all sorts of arguments to defend our faith. We can recite verbatim booklets like *The Four Spiritual Laws* and *Steps to Peace with God,* and we know "The Roman Road to Happiness" that, through the book of Romans, can lead a person into a personal relationship with Jesus Christ. But what God has primarily used in our lives to reach others is our love relationship. The Bible is clear: they will know us by our love (John 13:35).

We have led people to Jesus after they have gone out on a dinner date with us, been in our home and watched us interact with one another, or after they have known our family and seen how we handle adversity. It has been our lives, more than our words, that have led people to Jesus. When people see the obvious affection we have for one another—the walking hand in hand, the knowing touch on the shoulders, or the twinkle in our eyes and smile when we greet each other—they have wanted to know what we have. It is at that time we can tell them about the personal relationship we have with Jesus that has given us hope and the ability to love one another.

What happens behind closed bedroom doors is apparent after you step back into the mainstream of real life. You don't even have to talk about how sizzling your sex life is—people will just know it—and they will want it. So be prepared: your red-hot monogamy is a bright beacon for those soul ships being tossed about by the storms of life.

How to be a Creative Lover

God created the world in seven days, so it seems possible that if we are made in God's image, we might just have a few creative ideas in our minds too. In our book *Red-Hot Monogamy* we list over two hundred romantic and sexual ideas to fan the flame on your love. But in this book for newlyweds, we are going to go one better—we are going to teach you how to create your own red-hot ideas. It is so much better to own the skill than to just borrow the equipment!

So here's the inside scoop on how to become a creative lover:

*L*isten

*O*bserve

*V*ary

*E*xtract

Listen

Your spouse will drop hints about the things he or she loves and you can use these hints to create more romance and sizzle in your relationship. For example, if you listen to Bill and me in a casual lunch conversation, you would be apt to find out that Bill loves:

• Football
• Ocean fishing
• Helping people figure out life and love

- To build
- To be active: work out, hike, bike, fish
- To cook
- To eat authentic culinary adventures when we travel
- To laugh and tell jokes
- Teaching the Bible
- His kids, especially giving them new, manly adventures

You would find out that Pam loves:

- To travel with Bill
- To dance, walk, bike
- Country life, the mountains, cabins, the simple side of life
- To laugh at Bill's stories
- To study and teach the Bible and church history
- To help women achieve in life and love
- Her kids, especially when she uses creative ideas to develop their character
- Classical literature, especially romantic poetry, Hawthorne, and British lit
- To go to the spa as a treat

It doesn't take much imagination then to know that if I (Pam) give Bill a day of ocean fishing or if he gave me a day at the spa, we would be more interested in each other at the end of that day. But it doesn't have to cost a lot. Walking is on both our lists, so an evening stroll is apt to also put us in the mood. We love to laugh, so renting a comedy or standing in a bookstore reading joke books are also like aphrodisiacs to us.

As I have listened more carefully to Bill's loves, I have found a curious nature that loves to explore local exotic restaurants. I have discovered that he loves books about how things work. If I really want to get his attention, I could create a bookmark that read: "When you read to this bookmark, come read between the lines of my body and see how I work."

All Bill would have to do for a guarantee of a long night of satisfying sex would be to whisk me to a mountain cabin, light a fire, and read a few love poems and I would be all over him.

Bill and I keep a running list of "loves" we discover about one another while listening. Make a file on your computer, or keep a sheet of paper in the front of your Bible so that when you have your daily quiet time with God, God can remind you of ways to listen to, then love your spouse.

Observe

On the TV show *Monk*, the audience is awed each week by the detective's keen skills of observation. You can become a detective and easily observe what will bless and ignite your spouse. Here are some things to observe:

- What raises stress in your partner—then make a plan to lower it
- What lifts the spirit—then make a plan to repeat it
- What calms the atmosphere—then recreate it
- What delights the eyes—then become it
- What discourages—then avoid it
- What things are collectible—then add to it
- When he or she sighs or purrs—then repeat it
- What makes him/her ask for more—then expand it
- What draws him/her to you—then protect it

Vary

Vary the place. The most common position for sex is "missionary," or man on top. This very common position will take on a new thrill in a new location: on a blanket on a country picnic, on a desk, on a patio lounge chair, on a boulder on a mountaintop, on the jungle floor, in a meadow, or on a pile of hay in the barn.

Vary your positions. If "missionary" is the norm, then "cowgirl up" and let the woman be on top for a change, lie spooning side by side, enter her from behind while she kneels, or try it when she is sitting on the bathroom or kitchen counter.

Vary the lighting. Candles, sunlight, broad daylight, by a fire, twinkling Christmas lights, paper lanterns, a lamp shade with a scarf over it are just a few ways to vary the lighting.

Vary the sensual experience. Use all your five senses. Hear new sounds, add new smells, textures, or tastes. Make it happen in water, on a bearskin rug, or on silk sheets. Or add in a new smell or taste: whipped cream and chocolate, strawberries or cherries, cocoa butter, or fresh flowers on a bed of rose petals. Listen to a CD of the sounds of waves, rain, or jazz.

Vary your invitation. Sometimes the variation can be so simple, so inexpensive, yet it adds a whole new dimension to your sex life. Send a fresh lei of flowers to the office with a note on the where and when to meet for a Hawaiian night; send a box of chocolates, but in some of the paper cups, place clues to the where and when and have the entire night be a theme of "Your love is so sweet."

Extract

To extract love, take an old idea and give it a new spin. Personalize it, shake it up, add to it. For example, because we are relationship communicators, we are usually pretty busy around Valentine's Day. Often we have to be at the NRB (National Religious Broadcasters) conference. No offense to those in Christian radio, but the NRB isn't the most romantic place to be around on Valentine's Day. We have decided, however, to make it romantic the years we need to be there. One year, Bill scanned the covers of all the books we have written and made a series of greeting cards with personal love messages that used the titles as a part of a pun. Every hour all day, he gave me a card with a new message and tiny gift. By evening, which we spent with media on a ship in some bay, I was looking for any private space of any kind because I so wanted him! I restrained myself (some) but when we got back to the hotel, he was very glad he spent a little time on the computer the day before.

Red is the color of love. One couple we know has a red tank top as their code for wanting to be sexually intimate. It all started when they were newlyweds and he noticed each time she wanted sex, she'd borrow the same red athletic tank top of his and wear it around the house so he could see just enough of her breasts to get very interested. So an adaptation of this idea would be to buy red things and send them back and forth to each other as a code that you want sex: red-hot candy, red-heart candy, red panties, red lingerie, red boxers, red licorice, and so on.

Take the everyday and give it a twist. Once, when we were really broke around Valentine's Day, I made signs on the computer and hung them around the house in strategic places. On the stairs I placed a sign that read, "You have helped me climb to new heights." On our bedroom door: "You have opened my heart to happiness." Years ago, Bill raided the pantry and tore off labels to make cards of sexual invitation: "You are 'Total'ly Hot." "I 'Wonder' if you'll have sex with me." I had never thought Bisquick, Top Ramen, and cereal could be sexy—but he found a way!

To "extract" love, put your imagination to work!

Learn from Your Elders

Couples who have been happily married ten, twenty, or thirty years have discovered the secret of red-hot romance, so ask them for their insights and advice! When we were newlyweds, we decided we needed to learn from those who were at the top of their game, the most successful at love. We made it a point to interview some of the "silver saints" to see what we could learn. Some of the insights they shared with us are:

- Argue naked. It is hard to stay angry when you don't have any clothes on.

- Do something romantic every day. Just be nice. Bring her flowers, wash his car, do the dishes without being asked.

- Keep him guessing. Try to surprise him with something sexual every week: a new place, a new position, a new kind of invitation.

- Have built-in love STOPs: Kiss every time you say hi or good-bye; say "I love you" at the end of a call, e-mail, or when you exchange keys or kids. We kiss every time we pray. It is hard to stay angry at someone you kiss that much. Dave and Claudia Arp, authors of *The Second Half of Marriage,* kiss every time they see water—and they also practice the ten-second kiss. So stop right now and try it—kiss as you count to ten!

- Make time to be your spouse's girlfriend/boyfriend. Neither of you needs another parent, but each of you needs a lover.

- Be a spouse first, parents to your kids second. Once the kids come along, what a child needs most are two parents who are in love.

STOP This week, sit behind an older couple at church and strike up a conversation or just observe how they interact. Invite a couple you consider happy and in love after at least twenty years over for coffee or dessert and ask them the secret to their long-lasting love.

The God Factor

If you really want advice on love for a lifetime, you want to go to the Author of love, God. We have been in relationship ministry all of our twenty-five-plus years together and we have read the journal articles and research. We have made observations from our counseling sessions. We have listened to the experts, and we've witnessed what works in our own lives. When you boil it all down, couples who have a satisfying soul-to-soul sex life seem to have made some pretty simple choices that add up in a big way.

Choose to Attend a Jesus-Loving Church

Notice we didn't say any church, but one that has certain core beliefs. We've read the studies. Couples who describe themselves as "evangelical" rate their overall satisfaction with life and happiness much higher than the average population does.[2] Their beliefs include that there is one God, and the Scripture he wrote is without error. They believe this God wanted a relationship with mankind so he sent his Son, Jesus, to the earth to buy us back out of darkness and bring us into the light of his love. All those who accept this free gift of love will be with him in heaven someday, saved from eternity in hell. Evangelicals also have the habit of getting involved in service at their churches and communities as they share these principles with others. Finding a church where Scripture is taught may be a significant investment in your marriage.

Choose to Pray

We all know divorce is rampant. But couples who pray together form a bond that's very hard to break. So instead of opting out of marriage, stay and pray. As we said earlier, Bill and I have never seen a couple divorce, no matter how bad the hurt and baggage were, when they committed every day to stop, kneel, and pray together in humility.

There is something profound about prayer. It gives you a glimpse into the heart of your spouse. Understanding and compassion are built into prayer. That is probably why couples who pray together daily also tend to enjoy fabulous sex lives!

Also add in times you pray for one another. One man committed to pray for his wife every day. At night, as he emptied his pockets, he would toss his car keys under the bed so in the morning he'd be forced to get on his knees by his bed. That became his reminder to pray for his wife at the start of every day.

One wife walks her husband to the car each morning and prays for him as they walk. Other couples we know have coffee and pray each morning. We pray each night as we hold each other and drift to sleep (or drift to sex).

Choose to Forgive

One wise marriage teacher said, "We don't fall out of love, we fall out of forgiveness." When we forgive, extending grace and mercy, we are most like God. When we "act good," we should expect good results.

• • •

We've mentioned that the fruit of God's Spirit is love, joy, peace, patience, and so on. If you lived all these traits, you'd be easier to love, wouldn't you? The way to keep the fruit is to allow God's Spirit to stay in charge of your thoughts, actions, and emotions. We mentioned that the soft whisper of the Spirit of God will save you from a whole lot of trauma and drama. If you'll just stay close to God, the Author of love, he will write a beautiful, inspirational love story—through you two!

The GIFT

Discuss how you can make the love you share more apparent outside the four walls of your bedroom. You don't have to announce you have a red-hot love life, but maybe there is a small thing you can do to pull back the curtain on the stage of your love and let people have a glimpse of the love you two share. Select something simple like:

- Using your affectionate names ("honey," "sweetie," etc.) when around close friends and family.

- Touching as you walk by (a shoulder massage, an arm around the waist, a hand in his back pocket, walking holding hands to and from the car).

- Speaking positively and with a smile when you make reference to your mate.

- Complimenting him or her in public.

Each gesture of love a person sees or hears is like one more piece of evidence into the courtroom of potential belief in God and in the possibility people *can* be in love for a lifetime. Plus, the little things—the small tokens of love and affection—will add up in a big way later in your own bedroom!

The ball's now in your court. Will you two choose to live to build love? On our wedding gifts to one another there is a simple verse: "We love because he [God] first loved us" (1 John 4:19). We figured that because God created man and woman, created love, and created sex, doing things God's way just made more sense. Want to join us in a lifetime of love?

Unwrapping the GIFT

Today, for your sexual encounter, select which metaphor/simile you like best for love and create a sexual experience that is a reminder of that principle.

Sex is more fun than an arcade: What's your favorite G-rated Xbox game? We bet it is more interesting when played naked. Or perhaps you can locate an old pinball machine at a garage sale—that's a nice, flat surface for sex and the ringing of the bells as you "score" is an additional mood maker.

Sex is more powerful than dynamite: This may need a little more creativity. Please do not use any explosives! Instead, talk about times when passion carried you away. Talking about your most erotic times together usually leads to making more memories in kind.

Sex is better than a Bowflex: Exercise unclothed in your room, or do an after-workout full-body massage for one another.

Sex is like a thermostat/thermometer: Have sex in a different temperature—in a steaming shower or in a nice cool pool or bath—or simply melt an ice cube over each other's bodies.

Sex is like a manufacturing plant: Some expecting couples enjoy sex on the floor of the nursery because it helps them feel closer to the baby they are so anticipating. (Not such a good idea after the baby comes though—let's keep it G-rated for the kids.)

Sex is better than X-ray vision: Sex can be so healing. Add the healing element by focusing extra TLC on your mate. For example, if she is worried, kiss that furrowed brow. If he is worn out from a day of working on his feet, add in a footbath and massage.

Sex is way better than drugs: Sex is supposed to make you happy, so do something outrageous that will make you laugh: sex with masks on (as in the movie *Dick and Jane*), sex while listening to a laugh track, or sex while telling each other knock-knock or other jokes during foreplay. Jump on the bed! Just have fun and play during sex.

Sex is like the Declaration of Interdependence: In the following chapters we'll give you ideas on how to bring spiritual aspects into your sex life, but you might want to start with something simple like buying a small lamp or candleholder that looks like a lighthouse, and light it when you have sex as a reminder that your love is a light to the world.

6

What She Really Wants
in the Bedroom

He's got that pleading, puppy-dog, "Mama, will ya give me some?" look in his eyes. Every time he walks by, his hands grab for you. You want to give in to his call for sex. You whisper in his ear seductively, "Be right back," then walk into your room to put on something more comfortable. There in the middle of the floor are his wet towel and his dirty socks and underwear—and suddenly you could care less if you ever had intercourse with this slob of a husband!

When you walk (more like stomp) back into the living room with your arms folded defiantly across your chest, you see your completely oblivious husband waiting anxiously, sprawled out on the sofa, looking forward to being completely pleasured by you, his beautiful (but now really ticked-off) wife. One look in your eyes lets him know sex isn't going to happen anytime soon and the sofa he thought you were going to make love on might soon become his bed for the night. He isn't sure what in the world he has done to offend you, but he is hoping it is repairable at this point. You wonder, *How can he be so clueless?*

Get Clued In

In the heart of each gender beats a longing, a desire, an often unspoken, unwritten code of sexual fulfillment. If you can tap into that underground current, you will have a sex life that will be described in terms like *sizzling, steamy, unquenchable, fulfilling,* and *revealing.*

You may find yourself echoing the famous Jerry MacGuire line: "You complete me."

Bill and I were newlyweds in the oil-rich countryside of Bakersfield, California. Oil derricks dotted the land surrounding the growing metroplex of a city. Many of our friends worked in the oil fields. At Bakersfield High, the mascot of The Drillers was an oilman. Drillers were in charge of searching out new underground oil fields, then drilling, often hundreds of feet under the earth's surface, to pull out the expensive, precious crude oil. As in many places in the eighties, oil money provided a healthy living for the bulk of Bakersfield. The economy boomed. Bakersfield became a flourishing oasis in the middle of the desert.

In the same way, when you tap into the underground current of love in each of your hearts, all of life will look better, and there will be an unstoppable power, an unbreakable bond in your relationship.

So what is this underground river of passion and delight in the heart of your wife and how can you tap into it? If you want the blessing, you have to tap into your wife's heart, underneath the surface of life, down to the core of how God wired her. You have to come to grips with the fact that God wired women with certain inner needs and desires. Once those are filled, a magic button is pushed and the floodgates of passion are opened.

To have a passion that builds over the course of your lifetime of lovemaking, you need to accept those unique qualities and work to nourish them. Don't complain that they are there. Don't whine because you have to go mining or drilling to tap into the passion—just strap on your oil field boots, son, and get to work!

It will not be easy. Just as mining for gold or diamonds would have you plunging into underground caverns, mining for the gold in the heart and sexual soul of your mate is going to take a little work. It may even feel a bit risky at times because you will be forced out of your comfort zone. Keep the payoff in mind: a rich relationship, a brighter-than-diamonds future, a richer-than-gold bond of unity, a luscious oasis of sexual satisfaction that will pump into the whole economy of your relationship and make *all* of life easier. (Just take it from years of experience: if you meet her inner needs she'll meet your sexual needs. It's a kind of automatic, heaven-made domino effect that you should be grateful for and work to perfect!)

Okay, we think we have you motivated—so let's go drilling!

Under the Surface of Her Heart

Women long to be cherished, truly loved above life itself. That's the heart of Ephesians 5:25: "Husbands, love your wives, just as Christ loved the church and *gave himself up for her*" (emphasis added). Jesus gave himself for his bride. He died for her. He went the distance to secure her future. We, as his bride, see the tremendous value in his gift to us. Paul went on to explain, "In this same way, husbands ought to love their wives as their own bodies. He who loves his wife loves himself. After all, no one ever hated his own body, but he feeds and cares for it, just as Christ does the church" (Eph. 5:28–29).

Paul is telling men to love their wives in the same way they love themselves. Care for her as you care for yourself. Nurture her as you take care of your own needs. The picture in these verses is that of a baby bird being cared for by her mother bird, who will do anything to provide a safe nest for that little one.

Value Her Dream

One day early in our marriage, we were at a stressful juncture. Bill had become a senior pastor at twenty-eight. I had set aside my college plans to work full time to put him through undergrad then graduate school, and we'd begun a family. We had also moved geographically to implement the fulfillment of Bill's dream to become a senior pastor.

Bill was committed to my completing my degree but was less than enthusiastic when I enrolled in two classes per semester. He had to cover child care while launching his new ministry *and* building a home for us in expensive Southern California. He quickly became just a little overwhelmed and very overcommitted in his mission of providing a safe nest for us. (He didn't just play contractor—he was out there hammering up the home piece by piece, and most days, even though I was pregnant, I wanted to be out helping him too.)

Every day as I helped on the building site, my heart banked up love for him. What a huge sacrifice he was making—sleepless nights, hard physical labor, balancing the responsibility of leading a church and our family—just so we could have a beautiful and affordable home. In my heart, each day as Bill hammered nails, he was also hammering that trust pipe further down into my soul until it reached that underground current of powerful passion. Even now as I write these words, my heart longs to give my body to him, to love him in the ways he loves to be loved. His sacrifice to nurture me, and our family, is a strong aphrodisiac!

We finally moved into that home. As you might guess, our finances, on a preacher's salary, had been stretched to the max. We needed to create more income for our growing family. One night, after all the kids were in bed, we had a heart-wrenching conversation about our financial life and future. Bill knew that I really wanted to finish my English degree and pursue a career in writing and ministry. We both felt the flexibility and options of this degree and career path would lend themselves to my being available to him and the kids. I would have more control over the hours I worked and I could do much of it from home. But money was scarce.

Seeing the numbers in front of me, I said through a steam of tears, "I will just quit school. I can get some kind of job. I was an aide in the classroom before. Maybe some school around here will hire me. Or I guess I could get an office job. I'll just take whatever I can get."

Bill stood up, came over, wrapped his arms around me, and said, "No, you won't, Pam. You have sacrificed for me, for my education, for my career. It is my turn to give now."

"But Bill, you already have sacrificed enough. You built us this home, you have gone without sleep, you have pushed yourself to the limit. I can't ask anything more of you."

"You aren't asking, I am giving," Bill replied. "I am giving you the same opportunity that you gave me to pursue my God-given calling and my God-sized dream. What is the dream God has laid on your heart, Pam? If you could do anything for God, if you could pursue his complete calling on your life and money were not an issue, what would you do?"

I hesitated. "I really feel called to write for women. I want women to find God and find love and marriage the way we have. I want them to see God cares for them and their families and their lives."

"So what would be your next step?"

"I would finish my college classes, of course. I am only about a year away from graduation at this pace—and I would want to go to a writers' conference so I could better learn the tools to get a book published. If I go to a conference now, then maybe in this last year I can work to actually step right into a writing career at graduation. I have read every book about writing in our local library. I have gone to all the Christian writers' critique groups, and they keep telling me I should go to this conference next week."

"Why didn't you tell me?"

"Because I know we don't have the money."

"How much is it?"

"Forty dollars."

We'd both just looked at the checkbook. We knew that forty dollars was all of the "extra" we had after buying food for the kids and a tank of gas for the car until the next pay period.

"Do it. Sign up."

"Are you sure?"

"Yes. I am sure. Things will be extremely tight for two weeks. And even after that, if you finish college, this is pretty much the way we will have to live for over a year. If you are willing to tighten your belt, so am I. We'll find a way to make this work. Let me take on the *how*—you just put all your energies into learning the *what* of being a writer, okay? I don't want you to shortcut your future and I definitely don't want to stand in the way of God's call being fulfilled in your life.

"Pam, I want to be the one to give your dreams wings. We will step out on faith. When is the conference?"

"Next Saturday, but it's all day, and I have the baby to nurse."

"I'll take care of that."

We both went from crying to laughing because nursing the baby was one thing Bill couldn't just "take care of."

"What I mean is, I'll watch the kids. What if you nurse the baby, then go to the conference? Then at the midmorning break, I will bring the baby to you. I will take the kids to the park, then bring the baby back at lunch. Then we can go to the beach, and I will bring the baby back at the afternoon break. After that, I will bring the kids home, feed them, and give them baths. You can nurse Caleb when you get home. Will that work?"

"You'd do all that for me?"

"Of course, honey."

He could see that I was still hesitating, "Pam, I know what's going through your mind. Remember, I know you. You are thinking you aren't worthy, or it's too much of a sacrifice—am I right?"

I nodded, so Bill held me tighter. He kissed me and he said, "Then, Pam, you just think of this as our teaming together. It isn't just for you—it is for us, for our family, for our future, for our ability to remain obedient to God. Pam, I want this for you. And you want this for us—okay?"

It was more than okay. At the writers' conference, when one of my fellow members saw Bill bring the baby to me to nurse and heard the story, she said, "Now that's what you should write about! The world needs a few more men like Bill!"

So I went home and wrote up an article as an example of the Ephesians 5 challenge for men to nourish and cherish their wives. When the article was published, I discovered I'd struck a chord in women's souls. We received letters, phone calls, e-mails—responses poured in from around the globe. Churches reprinted the article in newsletters. Women asked if Bill did mentoring or men's conferences so they could send their husbands. Other women sent moving stories of times their own husbands had sacrificed to nourish and cherish them.

I knew Bill's sacrificial act of overwhelming kindness moved me to want to love him unreservedly, but his example hit the core of women around the world. Women long to be valued in tangible ways. When a woman is loved in this way, she is motivated to respond by giving of herself physically, emotionally, and sexually in a "whatever you want, baby" kind of way.

Just recounting this story makes me want to hunt Bill down in his office, sweep my arm across his desk to clear the paperwork and responsibility so we can make wild, passionate love there. Or I want to plan a perfect date, one that is completely Bill-centered: his favorite food, his favorite activities, his favorite ways of having sex —an "all about you" date!

When a man sacrifices to give value to a woman for her dreams, he will uncap a geyser of passion.

STOP Your husband can't nurture or cherish your dreams if he doesn't know about them. And it is unfair to ask him to sort through your long list of dreams to try to figure out which is most valuable to you. So take a moment right now and share the one dream that would help you be or become a woman who can reach her God-given potential.

Reflect Her Value

At the core, women long to feel secure and safe, and your wife will feel that way and respond with passion toward you when you discover the power of being her "mirror." In our other books, we share a story from our honeymoon that has become a trademark of our love and is a vibrant example of just how powerful this concept can be.

I (Pam) had stepped out of the shower and was looking in the mirror as I began to put on my makeup and blow-dry my hair. I began to point out all the flaws I thought were in my twenty-year-old frame. Bill was sitting on the bed. Inside he began to panic. He was thinking, *Oh no! She's going to get all self-conscious and it will take the rest of the honeymoon to make up for this. I could do a better job than that mirror at reflecting back her value.*

So instead of being short-tempered with me, he came over, wrapped his arms around me, took my face in his hands, and said, "Pam, let me be your mirror. If you need to know how beautiful you are, what a great woman of God you are, you come see me. I will be your mirror. And if I have to throw away every mirror in our house to get you to believe me, I will, because from this moment on, I will be your mirror."

Instantly I changed from self-conscious to vibrant, alive, and in love! Bill's words to me on our honeymoon laid the foundation for our lasting love because he chose then, as he does everyday, to reflect back to me my worth and value from heaven's point of view.

See-Through Yellow Valentine

Another way men can sacrifice for their wives to give them value is to be free with compliments—help them move into confidence. I (Bill) started doing this on our honeymoon, and I've reaped numerous rewards since!

A couple of months after our honeymoon, Valentine's Day was approaching. I made my first courageous step into the lingerie department of a major department store. I was young—only twenty! So I did my best to flash my ring as I walked through the skimpy items that hung on the racks by spaghetti straps. I spotted a yellow, see-through nightie. I knew Pam would be a knockout in that outfit so I bravely took it from its rack and marched up to the counter, tapping my wedding ring on the counter for good measure.

I knew Pam would be drop-dead gorgeous in it—if I could just get her to try it on! The skimpy thing was a big step away from the long, flowing, feminine but pretty-well-covering nightgowns in her closet. She had a few more revealing outfits, but they all covered enough that she could (but didn't or wouldn't) wear them out of the house as short sets. This yellow nightie, however, was one outfit that was definitely for my eyes only. But my eyes would see it on her only if I had given her enough words of affirmation over the past weeks of marriage to get her to believe her own beauty.

This was a Valentine test! Not of Pam's courage but of my compliments. I sure hoped I had given her enough praise, encouragement, and positive strokes to build the kind of trust she'd need to wiggle into that little thing. I did what any red-blooded Christian man would do: I prayed—for a miracle!

Valentine's night came and we sat in front of the romantic fire in our living room. We nestled into each other's arms, feeding each other—much of the expected foreplay you'd expect of a couple on their first Valentine's Day. We gave each other sentimental handwritten cards packed with words of encouragement and affirmation. Then Pam had me open her gift, a nice pair of silk (but tastefully conservative) boxers. I then took the risk and handed her my gift.

When she opened it, she was gracious and said, "How beautiful!" but underneath the words was a "You've got to be kidding, it is so small" look. So I went into action.

Pam knew I loved her, valued her, and adored her, but convincing her of her sexual strength and confidence—that was a breakthrough God needed to make not just for me, but for Pam. If Pam was going to truly be a sexually satisfied woman, she needed to gain the sexual confidence that is built through trust.

Trust is built through expressions of value, in the form of sacrificial acts and words of affirmation. I was just hoping I'd given God enough to work with! Just for good measure, I began to give her all the words of encouragement my mind could think of as I caressed her, head to toe. Someplace along the path, I invited her to go try the nightie on—and she did!

But when she reappeared from the bedroom, she was standing with her hands covering some strategic points of interest to me. So I gave her more words of affirmation and she came running into my arms. She told me later it was the look I gave her that sent her running to me to make love to her. It is the "Everything about you is incredibly wonderful and amazingly beautiful to me" look. It usually comes in the form of a wide, kind of goofy smile with pleading eyes and a deep sigh as if the wind has been knocked out of me. It is not something a man can fake and a woman knows it!

The good thing is that God gives "the look" as a gift to us guys when we value our wives with acts of sacrifice and words of affirmation. When those two things combine, we are functioning more like selfless Christ instead of selfish us, and the results are amazing. We gain the ability to express the love for our wives that we feel inside and "the look" appears magically on our faces, inviting our wives to trust us.

Well, that night was a breakthrough for Pam and me sexually. I cannot even tell you how great it was in front of that fireplace after she ran into my arms, but I will tell you it has been great ever since. Pam found her sexual stride that night and it has been a privilege to be her lover over the many years we have spent together.

A Word from (and for) the Wife

I (Pam) would like to add something. Bill's consistent acts of sacrifice laid a foundation of value in my heart and soul. His lavish words of affirmation given first on our honeymoon with the mirror metaphor and then with the tiny yellow Valentine gift have reaped long-lasting benefits in his life too. Not only did I want to love Bill the way he always dreamed of, those words of encouragement stayed with me. Any reference to a mirror, or my just looking into the mirror each morning, makes me want him. He has gotten a lot of sexual mileage out of those two early acts of love.

For example, he will sometimes slip a mirror onto the podium of a place I am speaking at with a note written on it in lipstick. You know exactly what happens for him the first night I see him after a "mirror moment." Every time I hear the mirror song, I want to give myself to Bill once again.

Because of the investments Bill made in me with praise and encouragement, I am free to openly and courageously love him. I have gained the confidence to step out and experiment a bit and I seek to please Bill by asking, "How would you like it tonight, baby?" And all we have to do is see anything yellow and ask, "Remember that first Valentine's Day?" and we are both instantly in the mood.

• • •

When you express value to a spouse, you express love. Loving a spouse is like a boomerang. If you give it, it swings back to you and brings more expressions of love with it because you just can't outgive God, the Author of love.

 The GIFT

Give your wife the gift of complimenting and caressing her, head to toe. If areas of her body are especially sensitive, or if she is self-conscious about them, spend extra time loving, caressing, and kissing those areas.

 Unwrapping the GIFT

Take time to set aside a day to give sex in a way that is all about her. Plan romance in a way that says, "I really put some thought into this!"

See if you can come up with a way to connect something she loves or something she will see everyday (like the mirror) to the lovemaking experience. You might begin planning this process by asking her some key questions to gain some vital information.

Wife, even though you know your husband was given this assignment, you need to take his efforts as a great compliment because he is stepping outside his comfort zone and trying to create a special romantic and sexual experience for you.

Here are a few questions for husbands to start with:

- What is the nicest thing I have ever done for you?
- What things do I do to make you feel I have sacrificed for you and for our relationship?
- What have I done that makes you feel more valued?
- What things do I say to make you feel more valued—or more confident—or more loved?
- What are a few of your favorite things?
- What places make you feel the most comfortable and at peace?

7

What He Really Wants
in the Bedroom

Jokes that float around the Internet often best reflect the issues of the undercurrent of culture. Here's one we saw recently:

> I never have quite figured out why the sexual urges of men & women differ so much. . . . One evening last week, my wife and I were getting into bed. Well, the passion starts to heat up, and she eventually says, "I don't feel like it, I just want you to hold me."
>
> I said, *"What??"* So she says the words that I and every husband on the planet dread. She explains that I must not be in tune with her emotional needs as a woman. I'm thinking, *What was her first clue?*
>
> I finally realize that nothing is going to happen that night, so I went to bed. The very next day we went shopping at a big unnamed department store. I walked around while she tried on three very expensive outfits. She couldn't decide which one to take, so I told her to take all three of them.
>
> She then tells me that she wants matching shoes worth two hundred dollars each to which I say okay. And then we go to the Jewelry Department where she gets a set of diamond earrings. Let me tell you . . . she was so excited. She must have thought that I was one wave short of a shipwreck, but I don't think she cared. I think she was testing me when she asked for

a tennis bracelet because she doesn't even play tennis. I think I threw her for a loop when I told her that it was okay.

She was almost sexually excited from all of this and you should have seen her face when she said, "I'm ready to go, let's go to the cash register."

I could hardly contain myself when I blurted out, "No, honey. I don't feel like buying all this stuff now." You should have seen her face . . . it went completely blank. I then said, "Really honey! I just want you to *hold* this stuff for a while."

And just when she had this look like she was going to kill me, I added, "You must not be in tune with my financial needs as a man."

I figure that I should be having sex again sometime during the Spring thaw.[1]

Why Can't She Understand?

When it comes to sex, you as a husband might have had an evening (or few) when you felt this way. You are grateful for any activity because sex in any form is a welcome gift. You know most of your friends saw the pace of their love lives slow once they got married. Thoughts are racing through your mind. They are more like questions, questions you are too afraid to ask, like: *Why can't we try this? Wonder if she'd wear that? I wish I could ask for this. Why can't I tell her what I'd really love to experience? Wonder if she'd think I am crazy or a pervert if I brought up that?*

You know that some couples have hot sex for a whole lifetime, but you wonder how they do it. You hope, wish, and even cross your fingers and pray you can become one of those statistics instead of the myriad of couples who break up over boredom, infidelity, or just plain stupidity.

Sex feels good so you don't want to complain, but inside you wonder, *Is there something more?* You hear bits of conversations from older guys whose relationships you admire, but they don't really talk about their sexual exploits in the golf locker room. You can tell, when they are with their wives, that some chemistry is happening. You see the wink, the glance, the way his hand caresses the small of her back, the way she slides her arm under his suit jacket so her hand can swish his bottom hidden from sight. She straightens his tie in a way that makes you think she wants to take it off instead of keep it on. Wow, you want what they have because you are convinced that behind closed doors, he is a very happy man. You just are not sure how to get there from where you are.

You are not at all sure how to even raise this topic because you don't want your wife to feel bad, hurt, or repulsed—because any one of those things means a punishment of no sex. You want to bring up the subject, but you aren't sure what the subject is exactly that you want to bring up!

All you know is that you fear the mundane, the routine, the everyday ho-hum of life. You want a sex life that is exciting, vibrant, and growing deeper and richer today than it did yesterday. But how do you tell her in a way she can receive it?

You wish you could find the words: *Honey, I want the feeling I'd get parachuting from a plane, bungee jumping from a bridge, hiking over the Great Divide. Sweetheart, I want the rush of driving on the Autobahn, racing at the Indianapolis 500, or hang gliding from Half Dome. Baby, I want the thrill of "hanging ten" in Maui, snowboarding in Aspen, or discovering the cure for cancer. Angel, I want the energy of jamming with the musical greats, the courage of a solider on the front lines, the wisdom of a president. Honey, I want it all! I know I might be going over the top here, baby, but wow, when I am with you, the whole world just seems better!*

When we make love, I feel that alive and that hopeful. I want to have sex that adds a new dimension to my life, a new spring in my step, and new boldness for my calling. Am I asking too much of you, my dear, loving wife? I hope not, I really and truly hope not.

I just wish there was a way to tell you that sometimes, when I am with you, I get the feeling I can conquer the world—and I just want that feeling more often. I want every moment I am with you to feel as if it could be our last so I will cherish it, cherish you, cherish life itself. Can you read my mind? Please, please, read my mind.

What Men Don't Say but Want To

She can't read your mind. You have to talk to her. To be sure, God designed you with strong sexual desire, but he also created you with a high sense of calling and purpose. When you tap into that purpose, all of life comes alive, including your sex life. Your wife cannot be your purpose, but God has given her to you as a kind gift to help you discover, uncover, then live out that purpose.

As you might remember, we've mentioned God has placed a desire for adventure in the heart of every man. The adventure is self-defined, so what you consider to be a worthwhile quest may be different from what other men dream of. God wants to lead you to the edge of your abilities so you must humbly and boldly cry out to God for help. This quest shows up in the bedroom as a desire to discover the possibilities of your sexual experience together.

As men, we can certainly get carried away with this notion, but God has placed in us a curiosity to explore the various ways of sexual expression that work for us as a couple. Since this is a male trait, your wife will never figure it out unless you explain it to her in a way that communicates respect for her and a loving desire to make her feel valuable to you.

Wife: Don't Ask Him to Play It Safe

Tom Cruise made his mark with a slide across the floor in stocking feet and underwear as he danced freely around the house because nobody was home. That feeling of being "footloose" is one that most men welcome. We women too often try to rob a man of his wild side of adventure. We seek to tame and train men. We act as if we prefer the gentlemen of English novels who act with perfect etiquette. While Bill and I are the parents of three sons whom we put through the rigors of cotillion and manners classes, we also applauded their sense of adventure.

Let me tell you why, as a mom, I spent equal time nurturing the gentleman in my sons as I did unleashing their adventure: every day in my office I see women who want their men to play it safe. These men had mothers who said, "Be careful." "Don't get hurt." "Be a nice boy." Then they dated girlfriends who said, "Spend time with me. Don't go rock climbing, play sports, or surf because you might get hurt. Besides, it takes too much time away from me." Then they marry wives who reinforce this safe behavior and say, "If you love me, you won't need to hang out with your buddies. Don't go hunting, come antiquing with me instead. Just keep this safe job; the consistent paycheck isn't so bad, is it? You don't have to spend all day golfing, do you? A week backpacking? What am I supposed to do while you are off river rafting? You don't have to work on that [computer, house, hobby] now, do you?"

I hear women second-guess every decision their husbands make. She corrects him in front of the kids. She complains about the way he does things around the house. She nags him about chores and bills and then disagrees with him in front of friends when they are out to dinner. We women, unfortunately, spend years taming our males, and little by little the adventurers in them shrivel.

They withdraw from life because it all seems so mundane and purposeless. They create a habit of coming home, flipping on the tube, and spending mind-numbing hours watching TV, reading the paper, playing video games, or surfing the Internet. The adventurers have died. They are walking zombies of their former selves, simply existing from day to day. They don't get in their wives' way, and the wives like this because now they have men they can control.

But then the kids get older, become teens, and get to be a bit of a challenge. These same women then scream at their husbands, "Get off the couch! I can't handle this alone! Why won't you get involved? What's wrong with you? Your family is in serious emotional trouble and all you do is watch TV? How can you just sit there with all this chaos going on?"

He sits there because he has been trained to sit there! His mom, his girlfriends, and now you have told him, "I don't really need you. I don't value your contribution. I don't really want your opinion or wisdom or input. I like being in charge, so just go sit on the sofa and don't get in my way."

Oh, I can just hear you wives say, "Oh, that's not me!" Really? When was the last time you said, "Honey, whatever you decide I am good with"—and meant it? When he made the decision, did you question him, correct him, and go behind his back to undermine him, or did you thank him for his leadership? Try it. Choose any three-day period and try only to say, "Honey, you choose. Honey, you make this decision, you do such a great job. Baby, whatever you decide is great by me because I trust you to be God's leader for this family."

I dare you—try it! It is harder than you think, because inside of each of us women, as we've seen, is a desire to control. It goes all the way back to the Garden of Eden and the fall of mankind. Part of the curse was "Your desire will be for your husband, and he will rule over you" (Gen. 3:16). "Your desire will be for your husband" doesn't mean that you will want to be all over him sexually—no, that would be a good thing! The desire is explained in the last part of that sentence: "He will rule over you."

See, the whole problem with Eve is that she thought she had a better idea than God (and Adam) when God told Adam not to eat of the tree of the knowledge of good and evil (Gen. 2:17). When Satan tricked Eve into eating, she was essentially telling both God and Adam, "I found a better way." And that has been the issue for women ever since: trying to find a better way than our men can find. Just saying, "You're right, honey" is like fingernails scraping a chalkboard to us. Why is it so hard to give them a little leadership respect?

God calls us to be helpmates, but too often we think we are helping by taking over. In previous chapters, you have heard us encouraging men and women to share responsibilities at home, with the kids, and so on. But there is a difference between sharing equally as wives and taking the reins and telling our husbands what they will or will not do.

If we want a view of a helper from a guy's perspective, take a look at how Robin respects Batman, how the crew of the *Enterprise* respects Captain Kirk, how George gives honor to "The Donald" on *The Apprentice*, how our vice president works to carry out the platform of the president. If you want a good look at what makes a man truly successful, look at how the people around him treat him. They won't be yes-men, but they will actively seek to make his dreams happen, to make his desires and ideas a reality. Is that your goal?

STOP It takes a strong, courageous woman to applaud a strong, courageous man on a great adventure. Stop for a moment here and see if you can learn about the adventure on your husband's heart. Create some space where he'll be comfortable. Put him in the recliner, on the bed, or on the sofa. If you have children, find a place for them to stay for a few hours so your husband will feel like the center of your universe for a change. Put on his favorite music, get his favorite snacks, and massage his shoulders or feet as you ask him some key questions:

- When you were a little boy, what games did you play? What did you want to be when you grew up? Why did you think you wanted to do that—what was the appeal?

- If you could go on vacation anyplace and do anything, no matter how dangerous, what kinds of things would you do?

- If money were no problem and all our needs were provided for, what would you do for a living?

- If you could achieve one goal by the end of your life, what would it be?

- If you could be in the "Who's Who" in any area of life or

win any kind of award, what kind of accolade or award
would you want to win?

Your risk will be to ask the questions, his risk will be to vul-
nerably answer them. In every adventure, there is a sense of risk.
The goal is for a man to find God's adventure for his life, and your
goal as his partner in this adventure is to ask yourself, *What can
I do that will show honor and respect for the dream? And how can I
provide the energy and encouragement that builds up my husband and
his dream?*

Applaud the Adventure

The adventure that resides at the core of every man will be reflected
in his sexual relationship with you. Leave aside any preconceived
ideas about what you think he might be thinking or desiring. A man
is always asking himself:

- Am I learning something new about my wife or about
  myself?
- Am I experiencing a deeper connection with my wife?
- Am I seeing a new facet in our sexual relationship?
- Am I experiencing a new shared memory with my wife?

Every man has a different definition of sexual adventure. If you
are wondering what kind of "adventure" is acceptable in God's view,
we can get some ideas from Scripture.

If you want GREAT sex, check out God's plan for an intimate
adventure:

Guard Your Sex Life

Your sexual interaction is just for you two. Keep the experience
and the act a secret, a private pleasure between just the two of you.
"Marriage should be honored by all, and the marriage bed kept

pure, for God will judge the adulterer and all the sexually immoral" (Heb. 13:4).

Respect the Power

The intimacy involved in sex exposes us to one another body, soul, and spirit. Sex encourages you to be in reasonable physical condition. It connects you emotionally to your partner in a way no other activity can. The bond that forms between you and your lover gives you greater understanding of the love that Christ has for the church. As a result, an active sexual experience will cause growth in the most important areas of your life. "For this reason a man will leave his father and mother and be united to his wife, and they will become one flesh" (Gen. 2:24).

Explore Your Style

As you continue to grow in your love for one another, you will discover ways of expressing your passion. Your sexual interaction will become a language you speak just between the two of you. You will discover that some experiences are a onetime affair while others become part of your sexual dialogue. Here's an example of a couple finding their sexual style, or the language of love in the Bible:

> Awake, north wind,
>   and come, south wind!
> Blow on my garden,
>   that its fragrance may spread abroad.
> Let my lover come into his garden
>   and taste its choice fruits. (Song of Songs 4:16)

Garden. Fruit. Wind: all pictures of a desire for love. And making love is a spiritual priority. Paul wrote, "The wife's body does not belong to her alone but also to her husband. In the same way, the husband's body does not belong to him alone but also to his wife" (1 Cor. 7:4).

Agree Upon It

The experience, the time, the place, the position should make you both feel comfortable and close. "Wives, submit to your husbands as to the Lord. . . . Husbands, love your wives, just as Christ loved the church and gave himself up for her" (Eph. 5:22, 25).

Take into Account Your Entire Life

Don't risk your reputation, your future happiness, your goals, your health, or your life just for a few minutes of sex. "A prudent man sees danger and takes refuge, / but the simple keep going and suffer for it" (Prov. 22:3).

God's plan for you two will be *great*!

Adventurer's Heart

Now that the basics are in place, God gives a whole lot of freedom and latitude in a couple's sexual relationship. You can set off on an adventure together. But a wife might feel she needs a little more information for it.

A man thinks an adventurous wife is a one who will:

- Flirt: Invite him into an ongoing sexual relationship.
- Flaunt: Dress in a way to accentuate the assets he most fell in love with—for his eyes only.
- Frequently say "Yes!"

Flirt

Give a wink. Whisper something sexy in his ear. Send an e-mail and invite him home in the middle of the day. Have the bedroom lit with candles when he gets home from a heavy business meeting. Run him a bath. Massage his shoulders. Lean over—just so—to get something off his desk. Slide your hand onto his lap under the table at dinner. Do the little things to show him you are interested in him.

These subtle messages are great, but nothing spells adventure like a bold invitation for sex in a fun new way. Look at these examples:

- Karee whispered to her husband on their wilderness backpacking trip, "See that mountaintop? I wonder what sex from the peak would feel like? Race you!"

- Trish picked up her husband on a rainy night at the airport. When they walked into the house and began taking off their trench coats, her husband discovered that under hers, she was wearing nothing but a pair of heels.

- Carol walked into her lawyer-husband's private office at the end of the day, pulled the shades, flipped the office door lock, and began to undress her very responsible husband.

- Pat surprised her husband by appearing in his hotel room when he was traveling for work. When he walked in from a long day of meetings, she was standing there in a new nightie with a bottle of sparkling cider.

- While in Hawaii, Kelly looked around and saw no one on the long stretch of beach, so she pulled her unsuspecting husband into the jungle for some jungle love.

- Trina and her husband were housesitting in a gorgeous home with a backyard pool. At midnight, Trina woke her husband and invited him down for a midnight poolside picnic and skinny-dip.

- Laura slowly unzipped her husband's pants as they drove along a quiet country road. As she stroked, she whispered, "Find a secluded spot, a field of daisies, a meadow—now!"

- Sharon met her husband after work in a borrowed pickup truck. In the back was a change of clothes, a foam mattress, a blanket, and a picnic basket. They drove to the top of a mountain, watched the stars, and made love under the open sky.

- Kelly tucked the baby into bed, planted the baby monitor by the Jacuzzi, then handed her husband an invitation: "Meet me in the Jacuzzi, clothing optional."

- Carrie rolled over in the middle of the night and began to fondle her husband. He gladly woke up for this reason.

- Melissa invited her husband to the rooftop of their building. As he entered, she locked the door behind them, pushed "play" on a CD player next to a lounge chair surrounded by candles, and they made love with a view of the city lights.

- The evening seemed pretty average to Terri's husband until she walked out of the bathroom in an outfit he never thought he'd see on his very conservative wife—who never wanted to make love except in the dark. All she said were two words: "Lights on!"

These wives have an adventurous spirit. Their husbands are happy men. These are women who have learned to ride the wave of adventure with their husbands. Instead of complaining about all the sports he watches, pull on a team jersey and matching panties and I bet you can move his eyes off the TV. If he's an outdoors man, ask him if he's ever thought about making love in a deer stand. Accompany that fisherman on a private ocean voyage, but set an anchor in the middle of the sea and enjoy some sunbathing and invite him to join you. If he is into computers, walk in, straddle that desk chair he is sitting on, and passionately kiss him. If you'do this completely naked, he probably won't even remember he owns a computer!

Flaunt It!

Every man finds a certain body type attractive. He married you partly because he likes the type of body God gave you. He is also attracted to the way you think, your altruistic spirit, and your deeply spiritual walk with God, but there is some physical aspect of you that lights his fire every time he looks at you! This chemistry is a God-given thing.

Early on in our marriage I asked Bill, "Which parts of my body do you like best and why?" Then, for his eyes only, I dress to accentuate those parts. I (Bill) know that every guy usually has a favorite section of his wife's body.

Some men love an ample woman, so cooking, sharing food, and dining experiences are sexy to him. Others like the long and lean look and are "leg men," so they might be willing to spring for those new heels. Some like the Marilyn Monroe–kind of curves, so something like a clingy nightgown worn to bed will catch his eye. It is a gift of love to share what he loves with him. Think of creative ways to tell him you are glad he loves how God designed you.

STOP Ask your husband right now, "What is your favorite part of my body? What do I do now, or what would you like me to do, to accentuate that part for your eyes only? What are your favorite ways I flirt with you?" Have him list his favorite items in your wardrobe. Your tastes might be different, so you might reach a compromise that at home you dress for him, and in public you wear what you feel most attractive in. (Don't be surprised if your man says his favorite thing to see you in is nothing! Go with it, and just move the conversation to "Then what part of my nothing is your favorite?")

Frequently Say "Yes!"

The National Security Administration (NSA) is the organization that protects us from invasion and attack. Men have their own NSA: it is "Need Sex Anytime." When a wife sees and respects her husband's desire and physical need for sex, his heart warms to her. An attitude of complete acceptance and a willingness to work with the way God wired men will protect your marriage from many "attacks."

When a man becomes sexually active, his body becomes used to the routine release of semen. With the buildup of semen comes a buildup of sexual tension. If a man goes too long between intercourse with his wife, he can become edgy and short-tempered, and eventually depressed or apathetic. But if a wife honors this God-created need with gracious enthusiasm and attentiveness, her husband will adore her.

In every man's body are two small organs called *seminal vesicles*. They produce seminal fluid—continually. They refill after each ejaculation, and as they refill, they swell (think of a garden hose with a kink in it—pressure builds!). "In a normal healthy man under 50, it takes 24 to 72 hours for the vesicles to fill up. While not getting release doesn't result in damage to the body, it can cause a sense of discomfort and make the fellow 'grumpy.' This is one biological reason a man feels a regular need for release."[2]

The seminal vesicles cannot release any of the seminal fluid except by ejaculation. Around the vesicles is a sensitive network of nerves that connects to a man's hypothalamus. The hypothalamus contains a kind of circuit designed to trigger sexual arousal. When the hypothalamus gets enough signals, it causes testosterone to be released into the bloodstream. This then triggers the man's conscious awareness of being in a state of sexual need.

If the level is low, a man can put his need in the back of his mind, but at a certain point, the accelerating rate of release of the male hormone into a man's bloodstream affects his mind powerfully and he involuntarily finds himself being intensely distracted by sexual thoughts and desires.

We as wives need to "turn on the hose" and turn on our husbands (by just being around and when we have sex with them). It is kind and thoughtful if we plan on helping them release on a regular basis. At one conference where I spoke, another expert in sexuality encouraged a wife to have sex with her husband three times a week—with enthusiasm! While I am not giving you an exact number here, I do want to remind you that your husband will be happier, more effective, more motivated, and just all around easier to live with when you meet this need—often.

Bill says, "If women knew how much power they have in the

moments or hours right after sexual intercourse, they'd want to give it more often." While I don't use this power in a manipulative way, I do love it when Bill says, after we have been together, "Pam, if you asked me anything right now, the answer would be, 'Yes! Sure, honey!'"

While you shouldn't give sex to get your "Honey Do" list done, you might find a natural correlation because your husband will be motivated to please you because you've pleased him in a significant way. I am reminded at this point of a line in the *Spiderman* movie: "With great power comes great responsibility!" God wants us to give this gift not for our own personal gain, but for the gain of our husbands and our marriages.

Remember, I called this need NSA—Need Sex Anytime. If you are too busy for regular, weekly (or several times a week) sex, you are *too busy*. Some simple ways to meet this NSA are: turn off the TV, schedule sex at least once a week, get a better lock on the door, get a better stereo system so you feel more privacy, or each of you take one thing out of your calendar each week and give that time to your spouse. You will get bonus points if your husband sees you are trying to create time for him!

Respect the Adventure

The gift of sexual adventure is a significant way to show you respect your husband and the way God wired him. A husband desires to be "dangerous in a safe way."[3] I (Pam) spend a lot of time with women. I was director of women's ministry at a church for over fifteen years. I speak to women's groups around the world weekly. I speak at marriage events and spend time with women there as well. And I have made an observation: we women are not as good at putting our men's needs before our needs as we think we are. I can talk a good game, but if I want to take an honest look at how I am really doing, I ask myself these questions:

- When did I last dress to please my husband?

- When did I last ask my husband what sexual fantasy he would like to try?

- When did I last give my husband a real day off, complete with zero expectations?

- When was the last time I took a whole day and said nothing but positive and complimentary things about and to my husband?

- When did I last ask my husband what kind of undergarments he likes to see on me? Or let him pick out my lingerie?

- When did I last shop for kick-around or sexy clothes that he might like to wear? And if I bought him any, did I ask his opinion first?

- When was the last time I asked him what he would like me to do as foreplay? Or in the sex act?

- When was the last time I complimented his abilities as a lovemaker?

- When was the last time I said in public how fortunate I feel being married to such a great guy?

In my seminar "How to Put a Smile on His Face: The Benefits of Red-Hot Monogamy," I tell women: If you want him to do well at that job interview, don't rerun all the questions and answers for him the way his mother would. Instead, make wild, passionate, "It's all for you" love. Make him feel as if he is the next Donald Trump, MVP of the Super Bowl, Albert Einstein, or whoever his hero might be. Believe in him and make love to him in a way that shows you believe he is the greatest lover, greatest businessman, greatest leader, greatest friend, and greatest father in the entire universe. Love him enthusiastically, energetically, and respectfully. You'll be amazed at the confidence he will feel the next day!

• • •

If we truly want husbands who feel as if they can rule the world, then behind closed doors we should seek to make them feel like kings. It follows, then, women who treat their husbands like kings will be made to feel like queens.

 ## The GIFT

Earlier in the chapter I (Pam) encouraged wives to ask questions to discover their husbands' adventures. Now be brave enough to ask, "What can we do as a couple to help you move closer to the fulfillment of your adventure?"

 ## Unwrapping the GIFT

Use the answers your husband gives to the questions in this chapter to create a sexual evening especially for him. Begin the event with a creative invitation: send a key tied to a balloon in his briefcase; mail something skimpy with a note to his office (marked "Personal"); send an e-mail or greeting card with a list of all the places you have made love that you really enjoyed and add to the bottom of the list, "You made me feel loved all these times. Now I want to make you feel as loved. Meet me at. . . ."

8

Guarding the Gift

Sheila reached across the bed for her husband. It was the middle of the night and his side was cold and empty. Sheila pulled her weary body from bed and wandered through the pitch-black house, rubbing her sleepy eyes. As she walked down the stairs, she could see the familiar glow of Brad's computer.

It's three in the morning! she thought. *What's he doing working at this hour?* Brad was a talented, driven executive quickly rising in the ranks at his corporation because he was known for his dedication. But as she moved closer, she could see over Brad's shoulder. It was not work on his glowing laptop screen but images of nude women. Brad, who was gratifying himself, seemed almost mesmerized, not even aware she was in the room just a few feet away.

Sheila felt a wave of mixed emotions: nausea, anger, fear, hurt, and pain all swirled in her body. This couldn't be happening to her—to them—to Brad. Brad was one of the good guys. He was in leadership at church, he took flack in high school and college for not partying, but there he sat, the evidence of his indiscretion open for her to see.

Sheila's emotions were like a tidal wave. The waters of betrayal, unbelief, and fears rose until she could no longer hold back their torrent. As she wiped away the cascade of tears, she blurted out the question millions of women have asked, "What are you doing?"

Good Guys Get Grabbed

Like many other women, Sheila agonized over the question, *How can my husband—a good man—be involved in this?* One has only to watch one TV special on Internet predators to see that porn has its tentacles around men from every walk of life: young students, college athletes, successful businessmen, grandfathers, truck drivers, and government law agents. Look at the statistics:

> At $12 billion a year, the revenues of the porn industry in the U.S. are bigger than the NFL, NBA and Major League Baseball combined. Worldwide porn sales are reported to be $57 billion. To put this in perspective, Microsoft, who sells the operating system used on most of the computers in the world (in addition to other software), reported sales of $36.8 billion in 2004.[1]

The porn industry is merciless. The creators of pornography know that 77 percent of online visitors to adult content sites are male.[2] It is a massive industry that spends enormous amounts of money every day trying to get around the computer walls good-hearted men have placed on their computers. But the battle cannot be won solely with higher walls of technology; success requires higher walls of integrity, self-discipline, and understanding.

A Note to Women

Porn is one of the major killers of relationships today. Many experts in marriage and sexuality have become our friends and colaborers in this battle to rescue the sex lives of couples from the all out attack from the porn industry. In testimony at the May 19, 2005, Summit on Pornography and Violence Against Women and Children, Daniel Weiss, the senior analyst for media and sexuality at Focus on the Family said:

Dr. Patrick Carnes, a leading researcher on sex addiction, estimates that 3 to 6 percent of Americans are sexually addicted. That's as many as 20 million people. This epidemic isn't confined to individuals, however. Pornography is one of the leading causes of family breakdown today. Two-thirds of the divorce lawyers attending a 2002 meeting of the American Academy of Matrimonial Lawyers said excessive interest in online porn contributed to more than half of the divorces they handled that year.[3]

It used to be that if a man wanted pornography, he had to drive out of his way to a seedy part of town, walk into an adult bookstore, and purchase a magazine, book, video, or "peep show." He would then have to get in his car and drive back home. But today, porn is piped into our houses via the Internet with the same ease as electricity or propane. Porn is so readily available that even good men (and women) doing innocent searches can be bombarded with "cookies," pop-ups, or e-mail blasts luring them into the dark world of pornography.

And once a man puts one foot in the net of porn, he can be ensnared. Porn traps a man's heart and mind. He then needs more and more stimulation to get the same impact of arousal. To maintain the rush, he uses more and more, or he takes greater risks: strip clubs, porn DVDs, even prostitution.

By now, you may have broken into a cold sweat. You are thinking, *Pam and Bill, I see the stats. I hear you say it's a widespread battle, but I don't want it in my house! In our relationship!* Or you have already experienced the pain and you are wondering what to do. We'll get to that, but first we'll tell you what *not* to do!

It's Not About You!

We know it's hard for you to believe, but you have to trust us on this: when a husband is entrapped in porn it is not the wife's fault (no matter what lame excuse he may give). It isn't because you don't satisfy him. It isn't because you won't try things sexually. It isn't because he doesn't think you are beautiful. It isn't because you've gained a few pounds—it isn't any of those things. If your husband tries to tell you it is, simply say to yourself (in your head and heart): *I don't believe that. I don't receive that.*

Then, be calm. It will be the hardest thing you will ever have to do, but a calm response will be much more effective than an emotional outburst. Say to your spouse, "I'd like to explore the reasons we have found ourselves in this place, but I think we need a professional expert, a mediator, to best learn why this happened and what to do."

Porn is what many men mistakenly turn to when they are stressed or overwhelmed. The stress may be caused by real issues in your relationship, and those can be discussed in the counselor's office, but in the end, it is a man's own personal decision to use pornography. No matter what, his wife didn't "make him" do it.

Most men started porn use early in their lives. They innocently surfed the Web for their favorite TV star and a porn image of her popped up. Perhaps they were with friends when one of them discovered his dad's *Playboy* or *Penthouse* magazine and shared it with his buddies. In some homes, an older brother or father purposefully introduced porn into a young man's life as some twisted rite of passage into manhood. The boy liked the rush he felt. The next time he felt self-conscious, stressed, discouraged, or marginalized, he wanted to numb the pain of that negative emotion and he remembered the adrenalin dump of the porn. He ran to porn as if it was some kind of magic elixir or healing ointment. All he wanted was to make the stress go away, even for a short time.

Porn can initially provide the escape, but then it becomes a taskmaster. Porn is like a school-yard bully: every day it demands more and more in its extortion plan.

Pornography creates a vicious cycle of torment for a man:

1. A guy experiences pain.
2. He numbs the pain with porn.

3. He feels bad—guilt and shame hit (as they should).

4. He wants the pain to go away.

5. He seeks porn to numb the pain.

6. He again feels pain so he seeks porn.

One man caught in the web of pornography described its effects. He was on a trip down the coast, filled with natural beauty, eating at his favorite restaurants, and lodging at his favorite bed-and-breakfasts. As he stopped to gaze over the wind-swept ocean, he mused about the numbness that had taken residence in his heart: "I felt no pleasure. None. My emotional reaction was the same as if I'd been at home, yawning, reading the newspaper. All romance had been drained out, desiccated. . . . Was I going crazy? Would I lose every worthwhile sensation in life? Was my soul leaking away?"[4]

In some cases, the use of pornography so numbs a man that he can no longer achieve an erection. The very reason he may have desired pornography—for sexual release—becomes an impossibility. The best analogy we have found of what pornography does to a man and a marriage is this:

In Mexico and the tropical zones of South America a so-called "strangler" fig grows in abundance. The fruit is not palatable except to cattle and birds. After the birds eat it, they must clean their beaks of the sticky residue. They do this by rubbing them on nearby trees. The seeds of the small fig have a natural glue which makes them adhere to the branches. When the rainy season arrives, germination takes place. Soon tiny roots make their way down into the heart of the wood and begin to grow. Within a few years the once lovely palms have become entirely covered with the entangling vines of the parasitic growth. Unless the "strangler" figs are removed, the tree will begin to wither, dropping one frond after another until it is completely lifeless. The only way to stop the killing process of the "strangler" fig is to take a sharp knife and cut away the invader.[5]

Take Back the Territory

Satan is a robber! He wants to steal from your relationship and he knows porn will do it! But the devil doesn't just want to rob your husband—he wants to rob *you*. So he instantly plants all kinds of self-doubt into your mind the moment you see that your husband has been caught in pornography's grasp: *I should be in better shape. My breasts should be bigger, my hips more shapely, my legs longer, my teeth whiter. Oh, maybe I should have been more available to him sexually. I've been so preoccupied with the kids. Maybe I should have been more adventurous.*

If you let those thoughts take hold, Satan has won. When your spouse got involved in pornography, that was one loss. If you turn the pain and blame on yourself, that's two losses. If you keep blaming yourself or your husband, a wall will grow between you two in the relationship—three losses. If that walls grows, it will sever the marriage relationship—four losses. And if you have kids, they experience the fallout—now that's five losses. How many times are you going to allow Satan to win? To us, once is more than enough! So take back the ground Satan is trying to steal!

Men, it is just like a football game. When you got involved in pornography, it was as if you fumbled the ball and Satan grabbed it. Now he is taking ground, play after play in your life. It's time for an interception. Pray. Ask God to forgive you. Accept his grace, mercy, and forgiveness. Ask for his supernatural power to help you. Then, moment by moment, ask for the Holy Spirit's help. Place Jesus Christ as quarterback or coach in every area of your life.

Establish a plan to walk away from old habits. Get rid of any porn you currently have access to. Get an Internet provider with built-in accountability. Some sites and servers even offer the additional safeguard of e-mailing two or three of your trusted friends if you wander onto sites that you have indicated are "porn." Get counseling or join a group like Sexaholics Anonymous or Celebrate Recovery and find out the root cause of the emotional pain that is driving you to porn use.

Once you have calmed the storm, you will want to institute a long-term prevention plan. Get in a small-group Bible study where you can be authentic and learn to apply the power of God's Word to help you overcome old thought patterns and actions. Invest in relationship-building tools. Pornography isolates you, so attend a small group Bible study of married couples, a Christian Marriage Encounter, a marriage conference, or get some marriage counseling and rebuild your love life. Learn some new responses to temptation.

Jim Conway, an author who has helped hundreds of men out of the web of porn, suggests that when you see a beautiful woman or an image that produces lust (like on a billboard or as you flip through the TV channels), simply pray, "Lord, fill in my heart what I think that woman, that image, will do for me. Father, you meet that inner need of my heart." You can move the ball down the field under God's control. Every wise choice you make will get you closer to the goal line.

STOP Take time here to tell each other, "No matter what ever happens, I will always give us the opportunity to seek outside marriage help before I call it quits. I promise to give us a chance."

Don't Blame Him Either

You may be wondering, *How can something so personal not be about me—or be my fault?* The reason is, as we've mentioned, men compartmentalize life in little boxes. So a husband can have his "marriage box" and feel that you are a beautiful gift from God to him, then have his work box, sports box, his childhood box, and so on. Again, he may try to mask pain in any of those boxes with porn use rather than do something permanently helpful: figure out the cause and get rid of the pain!

It does no good to blame yourself for the entrance of pornography into his life. It is also counterproductive to label your husband. No matter how much you want to say it, no matter how much you might feel it, your husband is not a jerk, he is not a pervert, he is not a scumbag. He is caught in a brilliantly planned and scripted espionage plan. People go to great lengths to reel good men into the "game" of porn. And in this world, unless a man vigilantly watches over his life and sets a guard over his heart moment by moment, he may be porn's next victim.

Place the blame where the blame is due—on Satan. Then take back the ground Satan tried to steal from you and your mate by saying things like:

> Honey, I know you meant your marriage vows. You are a good man, but this is a wrong choice. I am not going to freak out, but we do need to talk about options to get you out of this world of pornography. It will rob you, me, our love, and our family, and I love our life together too much to allow that to happen. So, sweetheart, I am on your team. I want us to work together to find a solution.
>
> I am going to hand you the phone and I want you to call for help. Call the pastor, call a Christian counselor, call someone who specializes in helping men out of this trap, call a mentor, call your dad—you choose who you best think can help you. Either you are going to call for help right now, or I will start calling for help, but we can't just let this go. We are way too valuable for this. I love you and I will fight to stay in love with you.

Then hand him the phone. Hold his hand or pat his shoulder while he makes the call (or begins looking in the phone book for help). Flip off the computer (if it isn't off already), then sit down and pray. Choose to team up together to combat pornography instead of allowing Satan to use it as a wedge to break up your marriage.

If you become a brave, courageous wife and speak the truth in love to your husband, you will see one of two things happen in the days and weeks to come. First, he will go for help to handle hidden pain or an unresolved issue from his youth that is causing the underlying stress. You will see him gain new tools to help deal with some current work or life stress. These new tools will help him say yes to wiser ways to manage his frustrations, disappointments, and stressors. As he grows, trust will be rebuilt. Your relationship can then move forward if you choose to deal with the issue from your side and forgive by extending grace and mercy. You can choose to be a source of hope, comfort, support, and unconditional love as your spouse seeks to find his way out of the maze of pornography.

The other possibility is that things will get worse. He may go into denial and say, "It's no big deal" or he might try to blame you. Your relationship will deteriorate and his involvement with porn will most likely increase. If he refuses help, pray that God will bring him to the end of himself. Pray that he will grow dissatisfied with his choices, that life becomes depressing and unsettling. God promises to discipline those he loves, so pray God steps in on behalf of you and your marriage. Misery can be a great motivator, so ask God to allow the sin to make your husband miserable. You don't need to be a part of making him miserable, though. God has plenty of ways that are better than yours.

No matter which route he chooses, we have seen it is always helpful for a woman to have at least one trusted professional in her world to help her navigate her own feelings (hurt, pain, anger, disappointment, betrayal, lack of trust). A trained counselor, pastor's wife, or even a trusted prayer partner or mentor who may have had to navigate her way out of this same scenario can be your confidant. If you have a safe place to vent your feelings, you won't use your husband as the tackling dummy. You need to be able to process what you feel.

When you are with your spouse, you may need the courage to confront him or the compassion to help him in the healing and wellness process. Understand that your husband is one of many. In a survey of over five hundred Christian men at a men's retreat, over 90 percent admitted that they were feeling disconnected from God because lust, porn, or fantasy had gained a foothold in their lives.[6]

We held a "walk into manhood" ritual for our son when he was preparing to enter college. His mentors shared their insights on what it meant to be a man. Bill's mentor in ministry, author Jim Conway, said to us, "I am going to talk to Brock about handling lust." I asked, "Why, because most men struggle with it?" Jim replied, "Not most men, 99.9 percent. And the other .1 percent were dropped on their heads as babies!" It was an overstatement with a slice of humor, but a man struggling with lust is normal and his struggle is not a personal attack on you, his wife.

It's Not Just the Guys

We want to make it clear that porn isn't the only cause of sexual marital discord, and it is not just a male issue. More and more women are also being lured into the use of porn. However, it is more common for a woman to become addicted to *words*, rather than images, that end up destroying marital intimacy. The romance novel industry is booming. Over fifty-one million Americans read romance novels; 93 percent of these readers are women and most are college-educated. It is big business![7]

Before you conclude that we think all romance novels are bad or as evil as porn, we want to stop you. Some Christian-based romance novels can actually be used for more than entertainment—they can also teach great relationship skills. Instead of reading a novel for the reason of improving their relationship with their husbands, however, many women read to escape from a mediocre relationship into a world where the male characters are pretty unrealistic. When surveying romance novel readers, the Romance Writer's Guild discovered readers want a male lead character to be muscle-bound, handsome, and intelligent.[8] How many of us are married to muscle-bound men? Most of us have very ordinary husbands. When a woman reads more and more romance novels, her own spouse pales in comparison. And this comparison is so unfair that he can never live up to the hype that has developed in her heart.

Seriously, when a romance novelist sits down to create her lead male character(s), she will take the best traits of every man she knows and roll them all into one guy. What husband could compare to a man who has the brains and money of Bill Gates, the looks of Brad Pitt or the power of Governor Schwarzenegger, the romantic prowess of a 007 agent like Pierce Brosnan, a sexy voice like Keith Urban or the party appeal of P. Diddy, combined with the fatherly instincts of the dad on the 7th *Heaven* TV show and the religious fervor of Rob Bell, pastor of America's fastest growing church, Mars Hill? What guy can compete with that?

Images also affect women, though not as much as they do men. When I (Pam) was a newlywed, I worked in the home of a woman who was completely addicted to daytime soaps. I mean, she didn't miss a show. We planned doctor appointments around her TV schedule! I began to observe how utterly unrealistic the plot lines were. A beautiful woman would get herself in some dire straits and phone the handsome leading man, who would drop everything in his high-powered world just for her. He was always some multimillion-dollar business owner, but he could magically abandon all his responsibilities to run home to rescue her from some emotional drama. He had plenty of money to lavish her with extravagant gifts. He had all the time in the world to hold her and listen to her tales of woe and he knew just the right words to comfort her aching heart. It amazed me that these high-powered men, with perfect trim, sculpted bodies, had all kinds of time and money but seemed to never work! How ridiculous! My boss, like many women addicted to soaps and sultry romance writing, began to grow dissatisfied with her own mate.

In reality, men have jobs, worries, and responsibilities that are pretty daunting. On a good day, when they try really hard, they might be able to create a romantic moment or help with the dishes or the kids long enough to find a sane moment or two to listen to their wives' recounting of their days. If they are able to shout over the kids or distract the toddler long enough to get any time alone at all, they might just remember how good it is to be married. Rare are the times when a man has all day to be at his wife's beck and call to meet all her romantic and sexual needs and still have the time, money, or energy to lavish her with any kind of a gift, let alone an expensive one!

While men get entrapped with unrealistic photos of airbrushed women, women get ensnared with unrealistic images. A wise woman will ask herself as she reads anything on romance: *Am I learning skills to make me more content with my spouse? Or is what I am reading making me less satisfied with my mate?* If you are less satisfied or find yourself comparing your husband to another man, real or imagined, it's time for some new reading material.

● ● ●

If porn's poison has entered your home, you need strength beyond your own. You need someone holding you up so you can hold your marriage up. Invest in people and activities that will deepen your walk with God. Spend time with women who are courageous and who have fought for their marriages instead of tossing in the towel. You can't give strength and hope if you don't have them yourself, so take care of yourself—and you'll be better able to cope and to encourage.

The GIFT

Create boundaries to protect your sex life. Each of you list ways you can better keep your intimate thought and love life pure. Your sexuality is a precious gift and you will enhance it by protecting it. Here are a few examples of some choices we've made; see if there are any you might want to add.

Pam:

- I commit to not read any romantic story or novel that is explicit in sexual content (if it were on the screen, it would be rated R or X).

- I commit to put a novel away or discard it if reading it causes me to compare Bill to the hero of the story or to any other man in my world.

- I commit to not watch anything on TV that I wouldn't watch if my mom were in the room with me [or my children, or teenage niece—you choose who has a good, innocent mind that you'd want to protect].

- I choose to not watch couples have sex in a movie or on TV because I wouldn't invite people over to watch Bill and me have sex. Why would I want to watch other people?

Bill:

- I give Pam and the kids complete access to my computer and its history so my life is transparent and authentic.

- I will not watch any TV show, video, DVD, or computer image or look at any book or magazine that causes me to lust after any woman.

- I choose to keep my eyes on women's faces, not other body parts.

- I will not buy any magazines, books, or other material that would create a comparison between Pam and any other woman.

Unwrapping the GIFT

Instead of going for the fake images porn and romance literature conjure up, create some red-hot romance of your own. Talk about questions like:

- If Hollywood were going to make a romantic movie about your love, what location would you want it shot at: Paris, the tropics, on a cruise ship?

- What would your romantic encounter include: a quiet dinner for two along a river, a picnic in the country, a glitzy night out?

- What kind of music would you want playing in the

background as the big romantic overture that would
lead to red-hot sex: jazz, R&B?

- What gifts would be a part of the encounter?
- What would sex be like: unbridled passion, slow and
  sensitive, steamy and hot?
- Each of you take time to talk through what makes
  romance red-hot to you, then each plan a date to
  surprise the other with some of the ingredients you've
  listed. Why watch some other couple on TV have some
  wild, passionate tryst when you can create soulful sex
  that is real? Why settle for the counterfeit when you can
  experience the real deal?

Part Three

Figure It Out

Vital Info for Key Decisions

9

Decisions, Decisions

There are so many decisions to make during the first five years:

- Where will we work?
- Should we complete more education, training, or career development?
- Do we want to rent or buy a home? What kind of a home? What kind of a mortgage? Who will the agent be? (More on this in the next chapter.)
- Where will we attend church? How involved will we be?
- How involved will we be in the community?
- Do we want to be parents? If so, how many kids do we want to have? If not, what contraception will we use to prevent pregnancy?
- How will we deal with in-laws, single friends, married friends, extended family?
- What cars will we drive?
- How do we want to spend or save our money?
- How will we spend our recreational time? Where do we want to spend the holidays?

The first five years requires one decision after another.

The first step to being a couple who make good decisions is to surround yourselves with good, smart, reliable people. Life is all about relationships. You got married because you were in love. You concluded that you had discovered a caring, trusting, fulfilling, positive relationship. You didn't just get married to buy a home with your spouse and contribute to a mortgage. If home ownership were the goal, people would just have mortgage partnerships and it would be all business. But a life of love is more than business; it is a network of vital relationships.

Your Successnet

When you begin your life together, you will want to build a web, or network, of key relationships. The Bible says, "In a multitude of counselors there is safety" (Prov. 24:6 NKJV). You want to invest in these relationships because insight and wisdom from these key players will be very important to the success of your marriage, family, and the home you want to create. Because this group of people is so vital to your future, we will call this your *Successnet*. Who are some of these key players and why do you need them in your life?

Family and Friends

Family and friends are key players in your Successnet. Your marriage will grow stronger as you learn to forge new relationships as a couple with your friends and family, and in a crisis, they will be the first ones to show up. So nurture those relationships during the good times, and if rough times come, you will have the support you need to make it through.

Spiritual Advisors

Your pastor, friends who are in full-time ministry, marriage and family counselors, small-group leaders, and marriage mentors are some of the people who can play the role of spiritual advisors in your life. You will sometimes face decision points, tough transitions, and difficult circumstances, and you will want some people to help you discern God's view on the matter at hand. These key relationships are not made overnight, so the best way to have the spiritual advisors in your life when you most need them is to have them in your life on a regular basis.

Attend church and get to know the pastor (or some of the staff pastors). Join a small-group Bible study. Participate in men's and women's ministries. Involve yourself in parachurch groups that interest you both. (Parachurch groups are nonprofit, spiritually based groups that are not a local church, for example: Fellowship of Christian Athletes, Marriage Encounter, Mothers of Preschoolers.) And in a healthy family and friendship circle, often family members and friends can play a dual role as spiritual advisors too.

Health Care Professionals

Physicians, allergists, optometrists, nutritionists, OB/GYNs, personal trainers, and other health professionals who care for your physical bodies are all a part of your success. If you are young and healthy, you may underestimate their influence, but they will become more valuable to you with every passing year.

Insurance Agents

People never think they need these people until their houses are flooded or burn down, a tornado hits, or a family member has a health crisis or car accident, or, God forbid, a spouse dies. But it is precisely because life is unpredictable and calamities do come that we need to be wise and forward-thinking. As a couple, you need people who care about you and will give you sound advice on good health, auto, home (or rental), and life insurance.

Financial Advisors

Everyone needs to plan well for a bright financial future, and we all have to pay taxes—and we'd all like to save as much on those taxes as possible! To help you navigate the financial waters of life, you will need people in your life who understand tax preparation, accounting, investments, and retirement planning.

Lawyers or Legal Help

Friends who know the law—police officers, lawyers, and para-
legals—are the kind of people you want to be able to call, even in
the middle of the night if you have to, so you can make critical decisions if something horrendous happens. Some of us, because of our
professions, need lawyers to watch out for us in business transactions. Others of us might need constitutional law advice, and still
others might need help for family or futures.

Bill and I never thought we'd need a lawyer for the birth of any of
our children, but we did. We had obtained a new health insurance
policy before we were expecting our third son. We had obtained
assurances that the new policy would cover a scheduled caesarean
birth, since we knew it would be medically necessary. Upon the
baby's delivery the company declared it was an elective surgery and
refused to pay the hospital bill. A lawyer saved us from a huge financial challenge by defending our cause.

Transportation Dealers

Unless you live in a big city and take public transportation, you
need someone you can trust to sell you a reliable car at an affordable price.

Contractors/Professional Handymen

Once you own a home, you need people in the field of building
and maintaining homes. You will need to know people skilled in
plumbing, heating and air conditioning, gardening, painting, electricity, and general home repairs. A reputable contractor will know
all those kinds of people in your local area.

Realtors/Mortgage Brokers

When you decide you are financially prepared for home-
ownership, you need trustworthy people who will look at your current needs and your future housing needs, then get you the best
home for the most affordable price. Quality professionals in this

field consider your life goals and future dreams as they help you decide on a home investment strategy.

What Are You Looking For?

So how do you find these people? Is it effective to randomly walk through the yellow pages? At times you may discover a quality person this way, but it is not the most efficient method. The best way to find the kind of top-notch, quality professionals you will need is to know what you are looking for, then set a strategy to meet them.

What you want are people you can trust. How can you know that a person is trustworthy? Well, no test is 100 percent foolproof, because people at any point can decide to make stupid or selfish choices and leave us in the wake of their sin. For the most part, however, trustworthy people possess the following characteristics:

A Proven Track Record

There are several ways to discern someone's track record. Have the people (or company) been in business a long time, with few or no reports to their governing board? Do they have a solid reputation in the community among leaders and your friends and family? If they are new to the field, do they have track records you can look up somehow? If you are a newlywed and your friends go into insurance or real estate, you can look back on their work ethic while they were in school, even though they might be new in the business. Have they been leaders in your friendship circle? Were they leaders in high school and college? Have they consistently kept their promises to you and followed through on responsibilities?

Personal Integrity

Are they people who handle their own priorities well? Are they trustworthy with money? Do they treat their spouses and children with the respect and care they deserve? Do they keep their word? Do they speak honestly and avoid lying, misleading statements, or manipulation? Do they have a clean record with law enforcement?

If they did make a mistake or indiscretion, have they owned up to it and paid the fine or penalty? Are they willing to do the small things to earn your trust and business?

A Positive Work Ethic

We don't want to pay our hard-earned money to people who are not willing to work as hard for their money as we have. We look for the small things. Do they return calls promptly or communicate clearly if there is a delay? Do they try to keep a semblance of order in their paperwork? Do they give an accurate accounting of hours worked?

Passion

We have discovered if people's hearts are in it, they want to do their best because they want to keep doing what they love. We look for people who feel their professions are their callings.

Professional

Look for those who are successful at what they do or have the earmarks of past success in their lives. We first look for the people who seem to be the best at what they do. Sometimes they are too booked up or too expensive, so we go down the list until we find the person who is both personally available to us and a high-quality worker at a rate we can afford.

People ask us, "Do you use only Christians?" Not always. If we know a person's faith impacts his or her personal integrity (as it always should), and two candidates have the same professional integrity and proven track records, we will go with the Christian. We want our brothers and sisters in Christ to prosper so we'll often swing business to them. But if the best in the field is not a believer but meets all the other qualifications, we'll go with him or her—unless, of course, we see that person saying or doing something that is in opposition to our faith. If we feel the person cannot represent who we are accurately, we will make a change. Sometimes God uses us to fine-tune the professionals we use and answer their questions of faith as they answer our professional questions in their field of service.

Personal Accountability

Ask your friends, family, and professionals in the field whom they use. We have had the same insurance man for our entire married life. Jerry was the father of four kids in the youth ministry where Bill was a youth pastor. We knew he'd have to see us every week for years to come. We knew a good portion of his friendship circle and that his own kids were looking up to him as a role model. He is a man with the highest of integrity; his reputation preceded him and everyone we knew recommended him. When all the recommendations point to the same person, that is a very good sign.

Another example is the person from whom we recently bought two cars. He and his wife are a young couple. His parents are good friends of ours and loyal ministry supporters. They called him ahead of time to tell him to give us the best deal possible. He would have had to answer to his in-laws if he made a misstep, so we felt pretty confident he'd do a great job for us and he did.

Sometimes we use professionals whom we have helped in their personal lives. The relationship help we provide for a doctor, dentist, or salesperson can be a great motivator to him or her to do his or her best for us.

STOP Do you have all or most of the key people needed for your Successnet? If not, you need to talk about which relationships you need to build and when and how you will go about making those new connections.

Strategies for Decision Making

Once you have your Successnet in place, you are ready to implement strategies for making decisions. Often, when the need for a decision arises, marriage partners will battle back and forth with their opinions. Depending on personality, one person may always win out because he or she can just outlast, outtalk, or outthink the other. This kind of "winner takes all" decision-making approach is hard on a marriage because one or both of you may grow to resent the other for "the win."

Actually, in a "winner takes all" decision-making pattern, no one wins because the loser will do something to make the winner "pay." The payment might be the cold shoulder, withholding of sex, or some other form of withdrawal or manipulation. The resentment grows deep enough that a rift in the relationship occurs, and some rifts become so deep, so personal, that one of the partners just gets tired of rebuilding the bridge to keep crossing back over the rift. When a rift becomes so wide that it feels like the Grand Canyon, calling in a professional engineering crew (a trained counselor) may be your only hope to close the ever-widening gap. This "must win" attitude is one of the key reasons so many marriages fail in the first five years.

One couple Bill and I know is made up of a very strong partner and one who was more compliant. The more submissive partner was feeling more and more trampled on by the dominate partner's "winner take all" attitude. One day, Bill said to this very strong personality, "Do you want to be right or do you want to be married?"

If we hold on to our right to be right, we may win the argument and lose our spouses and our marriages. The satisfaction of the win is no replacement for a satisfying sexual life. Winning the debate will not keep you warm on those cold, lonely nights.

The way you make decisions sets the emotional atmosphere of your relationship. As a result, your choices determine how happy and successful you will be in your marriage relationship. Great decision making equals a great marriage. The natural outcome of a good decision will be that you will feel closer as a couple and more confident as an individual.

Decision-Making Strategy #1: Break It Down

Let's look at a decision Bill and I made the first year of our marriage: how to finish our education and establish our careers.

We had many options:

1. Bill finish while Pam works.
2. Pam finish while Bill works.
3. We both finish while we both work.
4. We both finish and take out loans and don't work.
5. We both work and save so eventually we can both not work and finish our education.

We immediately ruled out #4 because of the huge debt load we would incur. We ruled out #5 because we were confident that we would never get back to our education if we stopped then. We had seen too many of our friends try that, and they ended up falling short of their potential. The responsibilities of kids, a home, the extra cash to do fun things was too tempting. So we sat down and made a pro/con list for each of the other three options. Initially, we decided to both work and both finish, but I (Pam) discovered the learning curve of being a wife and running the home was taking more time so I trimmed my class load—so my pace slowed.

We knew we were headed to full-time Christian work, and we thought the church we were volunteering at would hire Bill after college graduation, but then a challenge changed our direction. Yes, they wanted to hire us, but they so believed in us and our long-range effectiveness for Christian work that they would hire Bill *only* with a *seminary* education. That meant three to four more years of education for Bill—and I still had schooling to complete.

We needed to regroup. The church offered to help pay for seminary with a scholarship, but that would cover only half the tuition. That meant we needed to pay for books, living expenses, and the other half of the tuition. Plus, we had to get us through our undergrad work too. We made a list of all the possible ways to get us both through school, then on to seminary. It was a complicated decision, so we had to take it apart piece by piece and make one decision at a time. Each decision led to the next. By breaking it down, we moved through the maze of options into God's will for our lives.

We were broke students, but we did receive some grant money. Since we were on our own, our parents' tax brackets didn't impact our ability to get financial aid for college. It was our measly little paycheck that allowed the government to give us more grant money than some of our single friends still living at home. But the financial reality of our situation played an important role in the decision-making trail we followed.

We needed money to fund the dream. We both worked full-time in the summer. That fall, Bill and I continued our education in the evenings, but Bill decided if he was going to get to seminary, he wanted to get there as quickly as possible. To do that, he needed a better job. He put the word out at church, and soon a call came in. A union oil field job was available. It was long hours of hard and dirty work, but it paid great. We decided Bill would take the job and continue in night school. In addition, Bill would continue to do some drafting work on the side since he had been an architectural draftsman before God called him into ministry. So for one semester, Bill would burn the candle at both ends.

To accomplish this, he'd need me to handle most of the rest of the responsibilities at home. I worked a part-time job thirty hours a week that paid well—more than my friends made working forty-plus hours. So I would give Bill lots of TLC and tangible help both at home and in maintaining the ministry we were volunteering in together for four months. If we could pull that off, we'd have enough in savings for Bill to take all the classes he needed to finish his undergrad work in just three semesters. Bill is a very bright student, so academics have never been a problem for him. We were convinced he could carry out the school plan if he could survive five grueling months of work, work, and more work!

Thankfully, with God's power and provision, eight months from making that decision, Bill graduated *magna cum laude* and we headed to Biola University, where Bill enrolled in a masters of divinity program. I continued to work full-time, taking a few Christian education classes each semester. The church gave us the promised partial scholarship, then people who believed in us formed a support team that funded the rest of the tuition. Bill worked part-time as a tutor to cover books and any other school costs, and I worked to cover living expenses. We eventually gained more grant money, so the last semester there I became pregnant and took classes as well. We then moved back to the church that sent us to seminary and Bill took a full-time position with them while he commuted to seminary for the last two years to complete his degree. We had two children by then, and it was my turn.

This plan of my working to get Bill established, then his working to get me established offered me the time at home to pour into my children when they were small. It also meant, however, that we were well into Bill's career and had two kids and a mortgage when it came to my turn to complete my education. I mentioned in chapter 6 how Bill and I approached my finishing my education. I whittled away at it and eight years from that night, I completed my degree (and we had penned two books, one my first book for women, *Woman of Influence*).

Decision-Making Strategy #2: Pro/Con List with Priorities

This is a method you might be more aware of. Draw a line down the center of a sheet of paper. On one side list the Pros (why you should do something), on the other side list the Cons (why you should not do something).With every part of the school/education/career-path decision story we've just told, we used these pro/con lists to make key decisions.

But this isn't a simple pro/con list. It is a list with a twist. After each item on the list, rank how important that factor is to the decision with an A, B, or C. Then compare only the A's on the list. Too often people think whichever side of the list is longer should determine the decision. It isn't the number of reasons on each side that counts. Rather, it is the priority of those factors that steer good decisions.

Let's look at a key decision that made it possible for Bill to graduate under the original time line and get on to seminary: what to do when the car died.

Buy a car

Pro	Con
We'd have a car to get places.	We'd have to take out a loan.
We would stop hearing my grandpa ask, "Bill, when are you going to get a real job?"	We would have to delay going to seminary to pay the loan.
Bill wouldn't hear people say, "You make your wife ride a bike?"	Bill would have to quit or cut back on school to work more either to pay cash or to repay a loan (if we could even get one).
	We might have to ask for a cosigner to get a loan since we have almost no credit history. If we asked someone, most likely one of our dads, there would be an emotional toll to pay.
	We can ask my sister and brother (who live in our apartment complex) if they will take us to the places they already go: grocery shopping, church.
	We can ask friends to pick us up for a car pool and pay them gas money.
	We can walk or ride bikes; we need the exercise.
	We can trust God for a car as a gift, so we have the chance to see a miracle.

Pro	Con
	We can ask the kids in the youth group to believe God for a miracle car too—and they can be a part of a miracle.
	Seeing God provide in tangible ways like this exercises our faith, which we will need since we are going into full-time Christian work.
	We can ride bikes with my brother and sister and develop our relationships.

After making the list, we marked the A priorities. On the Pro side the only A was: we'd have a car. The rest were just succumbing to people's criticisms and peer pressure—not good reasons to do something!

On the Con side, finishing Bill's education on time, no debt, and getting to seminary were all A's, as was the opportunity to see if God would do a miracle and have others join us in seeing a miracle. The Con A's were much more important to us than the Pro A, and the side effects of getting and staying in shape by riding bikes and forging a closer relationship with my brother and sister by riding with them more often all seemed like great perks.

For a year we rode bikes, we prayed, and the kids in the youth group prayed. My (Pam's) brother, Bret, and sister, Deney took us to the grocery store and church, and if they weren't using their cars, we borrowed them and just replaced the gas.

The week of Bill's graduation, a family in our church called, asking, "Do you still need a car? My mom passed away and we have her old Chevy Impala to dispose of. It needs new brakes, but I talked to Mr. Golden in our Sunday school class and he'll do the work for cost, so if you can come up with sixty-four dollars, the car is yours!"

We had sixty-four dollars! We had a car to go to seminary! We were part of a miracle that carried us into God's call for our life— and we are still friends with all those kids in that youth group who also prayed, and almost all of them are leaders in churches today. The fruit of a good decision lives far beyond the apparent reason for the decision.

• • •

The strategic choices we made in the early years of our marriage laid the foundation for our entire life and ministry together. What you do and what you decide in those first five years are a gift to your entire life together. Choose carefully!

The GIFT

> Take a decision you need to make, work all the steps of decision making, and come to agreement. Be sure to keep talking until you feel in love with each other—too many people end discussions and reach answers too early. If the answer doesn't bring you closer in caring and understanding for each other, then it isn't the complete answer yet.

Unwrapping the GIFT

> Have "Celebrate the Victory" sex! When you do the hard work to make good decisions, there should be a reward! We have found it motivating to reward ourselves (at least) twice: once when the decision is made at the beginning of the path, then again at the end of the path when the goal is accomplished. In the schooling example we described, wearing the apparel of the college of our goal and then stripping it off one another was a nice, pacesetting motivator to a dream. Equally satisfying

was hanging the diploma on the wall and having steamy sex under it in celebration!

We also decided that in all the hard work of education, the last day of every semester we'd have a special date in celebration of one more marker on the path toward our dream. We took turns planning these romantic markers, often using a copy of the front page of a graded term paper or the cover of a blue book to write the invitation out to celebrate and sending it to one another.

Each of you think of a decision you need to make, select one of the decision-making methods to use, and decide what kind of payoff you each want sexually when you 1) complete the decision 2) complete the goal. For the decision you select, come up with a creative invitation to psych up for the decision.

People gear up for a big game. Football players jump in a huddle or bang helmets on lockers; cheerleaders run screaming and squealing on to the field amidst a flurry of flips and kicks—these are signals that the game is about to begin. Do something creative and fun and invite your spouse to begin to dream about a decision that might be down the road but one you are excited to make.

And if you just really can't think of something creative—then "punt" and get him in his favorite workout attire, and you in the cutest close-to-a-cheerleader outfit you have in the closet, and create your own kickoff for great sex tradition. He can do a Heisman pose and you can do some high kicks or splits and see where the action goes from there. Use whatever you feel comfortable with, but do something romantically creative that says, "I'm glad to be in the decision-making game with you on my team!"

10

Creating a Home

Carl and Jessica live in the bustling city of Chicago, and as newly-weds they are not sure they can afford their first home. They want to get out of paying rent as soon as they can because they feel as if they are just tossing their hard-earned money into the wind each month. "Carl's parents are pushing us to buy something—anything," muses Jessica, "to get our foot in the market, but my folks think it is too early in our marriage for that big of a financial step. I know Carl and I need to make the decision ourselves, but it feels like the first really huge decision of our life together and neither of us wants to make a mistake we'll regret. We just aren't sure which direction is right or which direction would be the mistake!"

Kevin and MaryEllen want to move their family from an apartment into a home in the suburbs because they want their baby to have a safe neighborhood and good schools. Kevin thinks they can swing the mortgage on just his income so MaryEllen can still stay home with the baby. MaryEllen isn't so sure. "We saved up for a down payment when we both worked. We tried living off one income and put most of the rest in savings. I say 'most' because sometimes, in fact often, we used part of my income for expenses. Even though Kevin thinks we can make it on just his salary, I am a bit fearful. I want it to happen, for the baby's sake, but I am still pretty apprehensive. I guess if things got tight, maybe I could do a home-based business that worked around the baby's schedule. It all gets so complicated when you add in a baby and a mortgage!"

Shelly and Trent would love to move into a rural home with a lot more privacy than their apartment currently gives. Trent says,

"We can hear the couple next door when they make love, so we are pretty sure they can hear us too—that is a bit unnerving. And I don't just want to move from our apartment to one of those homes in the city with zero lot lines. If I can hear my neighbor's toilet flush and I know what they are arguing about, then the houses are too close together for my comfort level!"

Lisa and Tyler are excited to buy a home. In their midwestern city, homes are plentiful and affordable. As a wedding gift, both sets of parents and grandparents gave money so they could pull together a down payment. Tyler says, "We do really want to buy a home now, but the reason homes are so affordable is that we live in a small town and the market is pretty sluggish. We think we are going to stay in the area, but I am really new at the company I work for and lots of guys get transferred to climb the corporate ladder. I am afraid of getting us into a place where we need to sell the home but can't. I don't want Lisa to be stuck here trying to sell the place while I am living in some bachelor pad and commuting home for weekends. We know another couple this happened to and they couldn't sell their home for over eighteen months. The stress of living apart and making two payments almost wrecked their marriage. I want our marriage to be more important than our house. I also know I can't make all our decisions from fear or we'll never do anything in life!"

Chris and Yolanda just aren't too sure if the burden of a mortgage is worth it to them. "Why do we need a house that we own? Is a mortgage God's will for every couple? I mean, what is a house? Aren't we really trying to build a home around the kind of relationships and memories that mean the most to us?"

Do you relate to any of these newlyweds? For most couples, a huge part of their identities, and a big part of the dream they hold for their marriages and families, is in owning a house.

STOP Before you go farther in this chapter, use the following questions to dialogue about what makes a house a home and what kind of "comfort zone" you long for:

- The place I call home should be (select any that apply): urban with the culture, hustle, and bustle of city life; suburban with well-manicured yards and neighborhood groupings; rural with the peace and quiet of acres of wide open spaces; modest because I want to travel and be able to pick up and go; unique because I design it; affordable so we aren't stressed over a mortgage; large so many guests can come (or something else not mentioned yet).

- The favorite place I lived while growing up was_____ . It was my favorite because. . . .

Putting Your "Home" into a House

Many newlywed couples have to make a series of housing decisions those first few years. We moved eight times in the first five years of our marriage and purchased our first home in that time frame as well. So many factors can play into this decision:

- Current employment
- Potential salary increases
- Educational choices or degree completion plans
- The having kids factor
- Your current savings (or lack of)
- Current career satisfaction (or lack of)

These are all factors for both of you and your futures, so even if one is ready to buy and settle down, the other may not be.

One principle we have always lived by in our marriage is: *Go to the best.* If you are seeking advice on any decision, ask yourself, *Who is the wisest, most trusted voice I know on this topic?* Then seek out those professionals who have the most experience. It is a plus if you already have relationships with them in your Successnet because your trust level will be higher and it is likely they will not just give general answers. You will have the freedom to ask them questions specific to your circumstances so you will get better answers to your questions.

One of Pam's longtime friends is a Realtor named Cynthia Fenimore. We asked Cynthia to write up a few simple principles and some of the vital information that the average first-time buyer might need to make a wise decision. She provided us with the following information.

The ABCs of Home Buying

Buying your first home is an exciting and important step in your marriage. Not only is this a place to call home and have a roof over your head, it is a place to begin building your financial future together. Having some idea of the process can help you to manage all the emotions and activities that are involved with your home purchase.

Here are some steps to get you moving in the right direction.

1. Choose a Real Estate Professional

Choosing the right agent is of critical importance to your overall experience in buying a home. If you are from the area, ask your family, friends, and coworkers for the names of some good agents. The firsthand experience of someone who has gone through a purchase or sale of a home with an agent is the best kind of referral.

If you are from out of the area, look for signs of agents who are selling homes in the area you want to live in and call them. You can interview as many agents as you have the time and inclination for.

There is nothing wrong with letting each of them know you are interviewing other agents, but you don't have to tell them all. This is a personal preference. Just be sure that when you've made your decision, you communicate it to all you interviewed. They took the time to meet with you and it's just good manners and good business etiquette to let them know.

When you are talking to these agents, consider:

Are you comfortable with their experience level? While you may be comfortable with them as people, you need to feel comfortable with their level of knowledge. You need to be confident they know enough about real estate to be your advocate when things get tough. This could very well be your largest purchase for many years, and the results of your decisions will be with you for some time to come.

Do they communicate in a way that fits your style? If you prefer e-mail and your agent doesn't use e-mail, you are setting yourself up for some real frustration. If an agent says she responds well to e-mails, then test it out a few times. Send an e-mail and see how long it takes for a reply. If you prefer phone calls, do the same test.

Do they explain things in a way that is clear to you?

Do they give you time to ask questions?

When you do ask a question, do they answer it? At the same time, start a communication log where you will record conversations you have with your agent as well as lenders, prospective sellers, and so on. From the very beginning, keep a journal or log of some kind. It will keep you much more focused and effective and give you a ready resource should someone "forget" an important detail.

Accountability and resources are important factors in being represented and protected through the process of buying a home. If you have a personal, firsthand referral to a certain firm or agent, you should be fine. You may want to ask the person who gave you the referral why he or she liked working with that firm/agent. What is important to your friend may not be what is essential to you.

If you are from out of town, it may be best to choose an agent within a larger brokerage firm. The larger firms can generally provide more resources to you and your agent, and they have people involved in the paperwork. Always ask a firm, "Do you have Errors and Omission Insurance [E&O coverage]?" This insurance helps to protect you in the event of any legal mishap or difficulty both during and after a purchase or sale.

They should ask *you:* Have you talked with a bank or lender? Do you have any idea what your credit scores are? Do you have any money for a down payment? Have you been looking on the Internet for homes? These are essential personal financial facts that a good agent must have answers to so he or she can assist you in taking the next steps.

2. Choose a Mortgage Broker/Loan Officer

All right, now you've got an agent. Being realistic about what you can afford, where you can afford it, and how long the whole process takes are the next topics.

The key to opening the door of your first home starts with finance and credit, or getting the money to buy the home. When people tell you they "bought" a home, what they really mean is "We bought a home with the help of a lending institution. Now we've got the house, but we also have a mortgage bill to pay every month." Ask your agent for a referral to a mortgage broker or bank. Most agents have two or more they can refer you to. Again, ask family, friends, and coworkers if they can recommend any lenders from personal experience. The mortgage broker or bank representative is the person who will help you determine how much you can afford and if there is anything you need to do to improve your credit score.

A mortgage broker can look at many different lenders' programs and find a loan that fits your situation. He or she works with a number of banks and lenders to shop not only interest rates but fees and the terms of a loan. A loan officer, on the other hand, works directly for the lender or bank and has a limited supply of loan programs to offer you. Either one is acceptable but, just as in the case of choosing your agent, feel free to interview more than one for your loan. Be careful *not* to give out your social security number easily.

If you have good credit scores and have been at your job for two or more years, you should be able to become "preapproved." In this case, you can ask for a letter from the lending institution that will be included in an offer to buy a home. If you are not able to get such an approval, work with the loan person on whatever issues have come up and get yourself in a position to get one.

Please remember that not all loans are created equal! Shannon Wallace, the branch manager for Cal Pacific Mortgage in Escondido, California, suggests:

Be sure the lender has you fill out the entire loan application. That is the only way your lender can fully understand your situation and meet your needs.

Get a good faith estimate before committing yourself to a loan. The good faith estimate states clearly what your payments will be and the entire cost of the loan.

Thoroughly understand the loan program you are considering and committing to. Be sure to know your loan term, interest rate, and if there is a prepayment penalty. Your loan officer can answer these questions.

3. Start Looking—But Be Realistic

So now you've got an agent, you've got a loan person who has told you how much you can afford for a new home, and now you're ready to get out there and take a look around. Chances are you've already been looking on the Internet or in the colorful ads in the Sunday paper. Sometimes what you've been looking at and what you can afford don't quite line up. Be realistic when you find out how much you can afford. Don't look outside your price range unless you live in an area in which a buyer's market is starting.

It's a "buyer's market" when a seller is willing to be flexible on financial arrangements—he will allow you to rent-to-own, carry a second mortgage for you, or come down significantly in price. These are things that make it easier to buy a home, thus the term "buyer's market." Home sellers may be more flexible in areas that have a lot of homes on the market. The longer he or she sits waiting for a qualified buyer, the more willing the seller may be to come down to your range of affordability.

It is important that you be honest and straightforward with your real estate agent. Share what you believe you *must* have in a home as well as what you would *like* to have in a home. This will save all of you time and frustration. One of the things you can do without your agent is to familiarize yourself with different neighborhoods and areas. If there are areas you will not live in, let your agent know. If being close to work or school is important, communicate that.

4. Make an Offer

Making a well-thought-out offer to purchase a home is critical and one of the major reasons you choose the right agent. Every property is different, and a good agent will know what is best to include in the offer. There are some basics to this; your agent should provide you with a market survey of properties in the same area that have sold within the last six months. These properties should be in the same range of age, square footage, and number of bedrooms and bathrooms as the house you're considering. This gives you solid information as to what homes are selling for and how realistic your offer is.

A good home inspection can save you thousands of dollars and years of regrets, so be sure to have a thorough inspection done on any home you are considering purchasing. (Many states require this.)

Generally, you as the buyer pay for this inspection and you should consider it money well spent. If the home has a septic system, you want the seller to pay for the system to be pumped and certified through a licensed septic company. If the property is on well water, then it too should be inspected and certified by a licensed company paid for by the seller. The seller will need these certifications regardless of whether you buy the home or someone else does.

Other reports or inspections that the seller should pay for are the wood-destroying pest report (typically referred to as the Termite Report) and the Natural Hazards and Zone Disclosure report. (These reports have different names depending on what part of the country you live in.) You want to know early in the process if any issues exist. The title report is also a very important item to review—you need to know the details of the title report and how those do or can affect you.

A good offer lays out time periods in which these inspections and reports need to be completed by the seller and reviewed by you, the buyer, before your contingency period expires and certainly before the sale is final. Your review and approval of each of these reports should be made a condition of the offer.

In some areas, there are other issues that will need to be addressed through the initial offer and your agent is the best person to advise you on what those are. States vary in what is required and "normal" in transactions.

Before you sign the offer, you need answers to these questions: What are my obligations and possible liabilities if I decide to back out of the deal? Will I get my deposit back? Most offers include a deposit check that will be cashed once your offer is accepted. Know what will happen if you opt out of the deal for any reason.

5. Get into Escrow

To get into escrow means to get "into contract" on your home. You will be presented with numerous documents to read through, sign, and initial. It is imperative that you ask as many questions along the way as you need to be comfortable. A good agent will field all of your questions.

If your agent is unable to answer all your questions immediately, he or she should be able to get the answers from the brokerage firm he or she works for. If this doesn't happen, call the brokerage firm and speak to the broker of record (your agent's boss) and obtain answers to your questions. Make sure you give the agent enough time to get the answers you need before calling his or her boss!

If your agent cannot answer questions as you are formulating the offer, do not sign the offer until you have enough information to feel comfortable with what you are agreeing to.

Be sure that you get copies of everything you have signed! Many of the documents ask you to sign that you've gotten copies, so make sure that they do indeed come back to you.

Now the whirlwind really begins. You have legally obligated yourselves to do certain things by certain times. Ask your agent to create a time line with dates for these activities. Remember that you have a number of reports and disclosure paperwork to review, ask questions about, and approve—or not approve and cancel the offer. State laws and regulations vary greatly and it is best to go over what your obligations are with your agent before the offer is signed.

Stay in contact with your lender, the escrow company, and your agent. You are your best advocate even though all of these people are being paid to take care of your purchase details. My experience has been that the lenders are typically the weak link. Things come up at the last minute that they need from you or paperwork is misplaced. Work with all of these parties closely and keep notes! I cannot tell you how many times my communication log has helped me to recall what was said, who said it, and when they said it.

Why We Love a Fixer-Upper

We (Pam and Bill) would like to offer a bit of "been there, learned from that" advice. Our first home was a fixer-upper. It was on the market because the owners had died of old age and their children were selling the home. As sellers, they were pretty motivated. The home needed a lot of work, but none of it seemed major.

The benefit of a fixer-upper is what is called "sweat equity," which means a whole lot of work you do yourself and numerous trips to home improvement stores! But it is incredible the worth a home will increase with just a bit of elbow grease and hard work. So if you are at all handy, can paint, make minor repairs, or have a decorator's flair, it may be wise to consider a fixer-upper.

Even though we have remodeled a home, added on to a home, and built a home completely from scratch—the gamut—we have always favored the fixer-upper. A home that needs work gives you an opportunity to forge two lives, two styles, two value systems into one. As you both bring your strengths to the table, your relationship will be hammered together just like the two-by-fours in the walls. The time you invest in a home can also be time you invest in your relationship if you handle it right.

Just be sure, before you make the purchase, you count the costs. We have learned to make detailed estimates of supplies, time allocations, and outside specialists we need to hire. This has given us a better grasp of how much we will need to invest on top of the monthly mortgage payment in order to have the home and real estate investment we were looking for. We learned the hard way that most fixer-upper projects will take twice as long as you think and cost twice as much as you estimate! Once you get into a project, unforeseen issues always arise.

A simple example from our first home was when we decided to remove the paneling from the dining room walls and replace it with paint. When we removed the paneling on the first wall, we found layer upon layer of old wallpaper that needed to be steamed off, which added to the cost in rented machinery and longer hours on our part. When we removed the paneling from the second wall, the entire window frame came out because it had been eaten up by termites—a detail that slipped past the house inspector! What we thought was a simple project became a challenging pursuit—so it's good to factor in some margin in your time and money budgets!

When You Don't Want a Fixer-Upper

You may not want all the hassle of the fixer-upper if you have a few key issues in your relationship:

- If you argue over small details, fixing up a home will only frustrate you more as you have to make a myriad of small decisions.

- If you are having a hard time trusting each other with delegated decisions, you may not be ready yet for such a big project.

- If you have a major stressor that is already putting pressure on your relationship—finishing your education, a high-risk pregnancy, or problems with extended family, for example—selecting a less stressful housing option until the stressor is resolved might save your marriage. No real estate investment is worth risking your relationship. It wouldn't do either of you much good to pour your energies into a home that has to be immediately sold in divorce court!

Now You've Moved In

Congratulations! You (and the lender) are now the proud owners of your first home. Take pause and thank the Lord that he has enabled you to make this step.

You will need to consider some things after you move in that will serve you well in the long-term.

First, think resale. Many, if not most, couples will have some improvements in mind. Be careful not to overimprove your home for the neighborhood you're in. If you put too much money into your house—i.e., make your house fancier than the others in your community—you will not typically get it back when you sell. This happens because most selling prices are made by averaging the comparative listing prices in your neighborhood. Get to know what the neighbors have done to their homes and try to stay in the middle in terms of costs.

Another aspect to consider is how long to stay in the home. When you sell your home, it is important to talk with your tax advisor *before* putting the house on the market. You'll want to see how current capital gains laws affect what you will make from the sale. So be sure to speak to your tax advisor.

• • •

For most couples, however, the purchase of a home, whether it's brand new or you're starting with just "good bones," is a high point, a romantic cement to a relationship. If you invest time and energy in doing good research and getting sound advice, you can pray and talk through the decision with skill. You will find that putting your name on the new mailbox and moving your belongings into a home you have designed or decorated will be a precious memory in your love life.

 ## The GIFT

Spend time going on dates to look at model homes and looking at homes in magazines and on the Internet. Talk through what styles you like and what size home you need now and will need in the future. Talk through the real issues of owning a home. Who would handle what parts of this decision, and who would handle what parts of the home responsibility once you move in? Talk through what you can afford. Many newlyweds are younger couples who unknowingly expect to be able to buy a home as nice as the ones they just moved out of (their parents'). It is easy to forget that it took their parents twenty to thirty years to move up the real estate ladder to that home. So consider realistically: what kind of places you could live and still be happily married? You may even want to consider: *Do we want to consider relocating geographically so we can have the kind of mortgage we can better afford and create the kind of lifestyle we can afford?*

 ## Unwrapping the GIFT

The first few years of marriage, we made it a goal to stay overnight in many different kinds of settings, such as a mountain cabin, a French country bed-and-breakfast, a Southwestern adobe, a brick triple-decker condo, a cottage by the ocean, a country farmhouse, a high-rise condo with a city view, and a house-sitting adventure in suburbia.

Try making love in a variety of settings to see where you two feel most at home. Today, create a list of the types of places you want to try out sexual experiences and schedule the first one on your calendar. Then celebrate by turning your own current bedroom into a bed-and-breakfast. Prepare a simple breakfast snack on a tray for the morning, get a stack of home magazines and, after making love, cuddle in each other's arms and dream a little about the home you would like to someday own, or the next home you'd like to move into.

11

Freedom for Intimacy

You are kissing, longer and more passionately. He begins to unbutton your blouse, slowly, seductively. You long to feel his touch all over your body, so you lean into the kiss and respond by unbuckling his belt and unzipping his pants. You can feel the temperature of your body rise. Your body is aching to fulfill its desire. The kisses become more desperate, deeper, and somehow richer, sweeter as your heart races with anticipation. You can't wait any longer.

You tear at his shirt and tie as buttons go flying in every direction. Frenzied with passion and desire, you both move so skin touches intimate skin in erotic foreplay. You know, without a word, that you are just moments from ecstasy, fulfillment orgasm. Then one of you is jolted to reality and whispers, "Do we have a condom?"

Doubts fly, the same torrent of energy that you focused on each other becomes focused on finding that little valuable foil package, but none can be found. The heaviness of the decision and the risk of unplanned pregnancy is a sobering reality. The moment is gone—contraception has become an A priority.

While having sex is an exciting adventure, conversations about it are not always as enjoyable. The dialogue of values and pleasures that meet at the fulcrum of the contraception topic are a rich mix of practical and personal information that can lead to deeper intimacy, thus creating a richer, more pleasurable sex life. God created sex to go to the core of who we are as people, so the conversations we will have about sex and its natural results (possible pregnancy) will lead to greater personal disclosure, which helps us know each other in a more intimate way. So even though this chapter will have the flavor of a chat in your doctor's office (or gym locker room), it still can lead to greater sexual enjoyment because peace of mind in the bedroom is key to relaxing enough to truly experience orgasm.

The Basics

Just in case you were sleeping through your high-school health class, the need for contraception comes because sexual intercourse results in sperm that is ejaculated into the wife's vagina and travels up into the uterus. Once a month, an egg is released from a woman's fallopian tube, so if you time it perfectly and the egg and sperm unite, a baby is conceived. If you want a baby to enter your family, then break out the confetti and get ready to phone all your friends and relatives to rejoice. If, however, you don't feel ready for that "Rock the baby, keep it safe, build into its character, pay for college and wedding" step, you will want to have a discussion about contraception.

For most couples, the initial conversation happens prior to marriage, *but it is not a onetime conversation.* Rather, the "wait to have a baby" discussion happens whenever your circumstances change, you gain more information about your own sexual enjoyment preferences, and your reactions to certain contraceptive options alter. Even couples who are newlyweds and are already parents (as in a remarriage situation) will find the dialogue on contraception valuable as they consider the possibilities of bringing a new child into an already complex family system.

This chapter is similar to those Cliffs Notes you used to get through college English class. It isn't a detailed explanation of each option, rather an overview, plus a set of questions to help you converse on this very personal and subjective topic.

Crossing the Controversy

Just the mention of birth control within the context of marriage is controversial to many couples. Some feel that all contraception within marriage is wrong because couples should leave the number of babies they have completely up to God. Others feel that some contraception is permissible if the method prevents fertilization. This view holds that all methods that destroy life once it has been created are immoral. Finally, some believe all forms of contraception are acceptable, even if they end the life of an embryo (a baby).

Every married couple has to cross this bridge, discuss the pros and cons of each option, and decide what contraception methods they are or are not comfortable with. They'll need to test their conclusion against the question: *Are we willing to stand before God and give an answer for our decision?*

First, let's discuss the moral and theological implications involved in the decision.

Whose Decision Is It?

Is it completely a woman's decision because it is her body that will carry the baby? Two clear statements in the Bible give God's view on this. Ephesians 5:31 states, "The two will become one flesh," and 1 Corinthians 7:4 states, "The wife's body does not belong to her alone but also to her husband. In the same way, the husband's body does not belong to him alone but also to his wife." All this means that you no longer function independently from one another but are in everything together. Unity is the goal, especially if deeper marital intimacy is the result you are hoping for.

Unity obviously involves the two of you, but if you truly want the deepest, richest, most fulfilling form of intimacy, you need to invite God into every vital decision, including your choices regarding contraception. Some argue that a couple should never use any form of contraception and they quote verses on the sovereignty of God, and God as the Giver and Maker of life. But the Bible also tells us to "estimate the cost" (Luke 14:28).

For many couples, the cost of simply allowing nature to take its course is simply too high. A woman's health and the ability to pay for basic needs (food, shelter, education) of each child are issues that require wisdom. You don't want to find yourself as a family like the familiar "old woman who lived in a shoe who had so many children she didn't know what to do"!

STOP What is your view? Before you married, how did you conclude your discussions on birth control? Now that you have more experience in the realities of a sexual relationship, do you want to investigate other options? Do you feel a couple should just avoid all forms of birth control and let nature take its course, or do you feel some form of birth control is a more valid choice? Which shows more faith to you? Which shows more wisdom to you? Which will give you the family of your dreams or God's plan? How many children can you adequately care for given your educational, vocational, and emotional state in life?

When Does Life Begin?

With the inception of *Roe v Wade*, people have forgotten to think through the issues for themselves. In 1973, when the Supreme Court legalized abortion during all nine months of pregnancy, no matter the reason, it started a landslide. In the United States, over 40 million unborn babies have been killed in the thirty-plus years since abortion was legalized and more than one million are killed each year.[1]

We are each morally responsible before God for the choices we make regardless of how the Supreme Court or any court in any land rules. Science is showing more and more clearly that life begins at the moment of conception. With the advent of ultrasound, in-utero cameras, and other technology, we can see life develop from its first moments. Here are some facts abut the first few weeks and days of an embryo's life:

- The presence of a unique human DNA code signals the start of a human person. The egg and sperm unite and a new life begins. Nothing new is added but oxygen and nutrition. If the process is not interrupted, a human being will live about nine months in the mother's uterus and then after birth will live, hopefully, a full lifetime outside the womb. This unique person has never existed before and will never exist again.

- By three weeks after conception, the baby's heart begins to beat and blood pumps through the body.

- By five weeks eyes, legs, and hands begin development.

- By six weeks, brain waves can be detected.

- By seven weeks, the baby swims freely in the embryonic sac.

- By nine weeks fingerprints are evident—and never change from this point on.

- Between ten and eleven weeks, if an object is placed in the fetus's hand, he/she will grasp it.

- By eleven weeks, the baby's feet are perfectly shaped. The baby even has eyelids, hair, finger- and toenails. All organ systems are functioning. The baby has a skeletal structure, nerves, and circulation.

- By twelve weeks, the baby has developed the body parts required to experience pain, including all of the nerves, spinal cord, and thalamus.[2]

We also have some theological evidence for life beginning before birth:

- It is I [God] who put death and give life. (Deuteronomy 32:39 NASB)

- Did not He who made me in the womb make him,
  And the same one fashion us in the womb? (Job 31:15 NASB)

- For you created my inmost being;
      you knit me together in my mother's womb.
  I praise you because I am fearfully and wonderfully made;
      your works are wonderful,

I know that full well.
My frame was not hidden from you
    when I was made in the secret place.
When I was woven together in the depths of the earth,
    your eyes saw my unformed body.
All the days ordained for me
    were written in your book
      before one of them came to be. (Psalm 139:13–16)

- Before I was born the LORD called me;
  from my birth he has made mention of my name. (Isaiah 49:1)

- Before I formed you in the womb I knew you. (Jeremiah 1:5 NRSV)

- At that time Mary got ready and hurried to a town in the hill country of Judea, where she entered Zechariah's home and greeted Elizabeth. When Elizabeth heard Mary's greeting, the baby leaped in her womb, and Elizabeth was filled with the Holy Spirit. In a loud voice she exclaimed: "Blessed are you among women, and blessed is the child you will bear! But why am I so favored, that the mother of my Lord should come to me? As soon as the sound of your greeting reached my ears, the baby in my womb leaped for joy." (Luke 1:39–44)

- God . . . set me apart from birth and called me by his grace. (Galatians 1:15)

- Praise be to the God and Father of our Lord Jesus Christ, who has blessed us in the heavenly realms with every spiritual blessing in Christ. For he chose us in him before the creation of the world to be holy and blameless in his sight. (Ephesians 1:3–4)

Abortion, and a few forms of contraception, ends a baby's life. And it isn't just fatal for a baby, it is also dangerous for the mother. An induced abortion is:

> the premature, willful, and violent penetration of a closed and safeguarded system—a system in which nearly every cell, tissue and organ of a woman's reproductive system has been specially transformed and activated to carry out the function of sustaining and nourishing the developing child. Not surprisingly, any violation of the integrity of that system can lead to serious complications. Physical problems range from hemorrhage and infection to sterility and even death. Psychological effects range from depression and mental trauma to divorce and even suicide.[3]

Other complications from abortion may surface later.

For example, overzealous curettage can damage the lining of the uterus and lead to permanent infertility. Overall, women who have abortions face an increased risk of ectopic (tubal) pregnancy and a more than doubled risk of future sterility. Perhaps most important of all, the risk of these sorts of complications, along with risks of future miscarriage, increase with each subsequent abortion.[4]

So what forms of contraception end life? All forms of abortion, RU-486 (or the Morning-After Pill), PLAN B, and IUDs are all methods that wash a fertilized egg from the body—or end a life after it is conceived. The IUD is a small, plastic device that is inserted into the uterus by a doctor. The IUD generally prevents pregnancy by making attachment to the uterus impossible for fertilized eggs. It is our personal conviction that any form of contraception that ends life *after* conception is not God's will for a couple because God values life, all life, regardless of how many years, days, or hours old that life is.

Moving Past the Past

What if you have already made mistakes? In this modern world, it is quite possible you have already ended the life of a baby. Our purpose is not to inflict shame or guilt but rather clearly state what we believe is a very important and obvious teaching in Scripture: life begins at conception and all life is to be protected. So what does the Bible say to do if we have not held these beliefs or have not obeyed the conscience that God gave us?

First John 1:9 is clear: "If we confess our sins, he is faithful and just to forgive our sins and purify us from all unrighteousness." To confess simply means "to agree with God." The place to begin the healing of your heart is to kneel together as a couple and confess (agree) with God that your prior choice was wrong. Satan loves to gain a foothold, so when you pray, also ask God to break all bonds or footholds Satan might have gained in your lives through your disobedience. Then thank God that he has cleansed you and ask him for a fresh start. Ask him to keep the past from being a threat to a happy future. Couples we know who have taken this courageous step together have formed a stronger bond with each other and with God. Their humility has placed themselves in a position where God can once again bless them as a couple.

Hormonal Types of Birth Control

Hormonal regulated contraception is the most popular form of birth control because it seems to give a sense of freedom at least during the sexual act. There are many forms of hormonal manipulators.[5] These hormone-based forms of contraception are rated over 90 percent effective depending on user faithfulness.

The Pill (approximately 99 percent effective)[6]

For many couples, "the pill" brings the sexual freedom they are looking for. Many women take the combo pill, which releases estrogen and progestogen. The pill works by hindering ovulation. There is also a progestogen-only version, which thickens the mucus at the entrance to the womb. This is hard for sperm to get through, and it changes the environment of the womb to lower opportunity for egg to implant.

Both forms of the pill have a very high effectiveness rating, but it isn't perfect because people are not perfect. A woman needs to remember to take it daily! If you can remember your vitamins, you can remember something that will help you have sexual freedom!

The Patch (99 percent effective)[7]

The patch is worn three of four weeks each month. The patch dispenses hormones that seep through the pores of your skin. It is worn in several discreet places like buttocks, upper torso, upper arm, or abdomen. You can still bathe, swim, or exercise as usual.

Surgical Implants (99 percent effective)[8]

A thin plastic rod is implanted in a woman's arm and releases hormones for up to three years. The side effects can be similar to those of the pill or patch but also might include some menstrual irregularities or breakthrough bleeding.

NuvaRing (99 percent effective)[9]

This is a small plastic flexible ring that is inserted into the vagina and held in place for three weeks releasing hormones. It is removed for one week (during the woman's period), then the process begins again. If all works well, the ring stays in place for three weeks, but if the ring slips out, it must be replaced in three hours for protection from pregnancy to occur.

Injections (99 percent effective)[10]

Your doctor gives you hormonal injections every three months. In between, there is nothing to remember, but you do need to make your doctor appointments regularly. Spotting or breakthrough bleeding can be a side effect, as can weight gain or a delay when you want conception to occur. When you do want pregnancy to occur, you will need to wait a full three months for the effects to work out of your system.

With all hormonal-based birth control, side effects can include nausea, breast tenderness, headache, weight gain, and abdominal pain. For some women, there may be more severe health risks involved in using hormonal birth control; always check with your doctor for your personal risk factors. It is primarily because of women's negative reactions to the side effects of hormones that they explore other options. Do your homework. Talk to physicians and leaders you trust so you can make an informed decision.

Barrier Methods

These birth control methods are like a wall or shield to keep the sperm and egg apart and are some of the least expensive and most common forms of birth control. They function much like that overbearing father who flipped on the porch light right before your boyfriend zoomed in for the good-night kiss.

Gels and Foams

Gels and foams destroy sperm. Because of their lower success rate, you shouldn't rely on these products alone to prevent pregnancy but use them along with other methods, such as condoms or diaphragms. The downside is that some people have an allergic reaction to spermicides—and a strong reaction would definitely put a damper on your sex life if that were to happen.

Male Condom (approximately 98 percent effective)[11]

The condom is a widely used form of birth control made of latex or polyurethane. It holds the semen after the man ejaculates. Condoms come in all colors, tastes, with all kinds of textures (ribbed, non-ribbed), and are very affordable. Some men feel completely comfortable using them, while others say using a condom lowers their sexual enjoyment and pleasure. With a good attitude, using a condom can be a pleasurable form of couple bonding because the wife can make it part of her foreplay to place the condom on her husband.

Female Condom (approximately 95 percent effective)[12]

This form of contraception has been around for over a decade. Made of polyurethane, the female condom covers the cervix. It can be tricky to insert properly. A woman may need to practice inserting it a few times before she gets the hang of it. You might want to experiment to see which condom user makes for the best sex: male or female.

Cervical Caps and Diaphragms (approximately 92–96 percent effective)[13]

Cervical caps and diaphragms, often used with spermicides, also keep semen from reaching the cervix. You must be fitted for these by a physician or nurse. The woman must insert the cap or diaphragm prior to sex and keep it in for several hours after. So it becomes a trick to guess when you might be in the mood enough to require inserting the diaphragm. If you have used tampons or the Instead form of feminine protection (which is like a cervical cap or cup), you may be comfortable and knowledgeable enough with your own body to easily adapt and use these barrier methods of birth control. If you have already had children, these forms of contraception may not be as effective. The diaphragm and cervical cap can last years if properly cared for, thus making them pretty affordable. While they have some drawbacks, this is a suitable contraceptive option for women who are unable to (or uncomfortable with) using hormonal methods like the pill, patch, and injections.

More methods of contraception are being created year after year, so always consult your physician about the most recent options, how they work, and what their side effects may be. Then decide together which fits within the framework you have prayed and decided before God that is best for your future, your family and your relationship with God and each other.

Natural Family Planning (up to 98 percent effective)[14]

This method has many names—the Rhythm Method, the Safe Period Method—and has often been associated with the Catholic Church, even though people from all religions have used it. Couples who use this method have intercourse only when the woman isn't fertile (ovulating). Learning how to discern when ovulation is occurring may require a doctor's instruction. If a woman's cycle is regular and reliable, this method is easier to implement. It can be very effective if practiced with accuracy and self-discipline.

We will share just a personal thought on this method. After being very frustrated the first few years of our marriage with trying several different methods of contraception (the side effects were too uncomfortable, or the method interfered with our intimacy), we decided to learn about natural family planning. We were at a place that a baby would be difficult on us financially (we were still in grad school). We weren't sure if we could figure out the Natural Family Planning Method and be disciplined enough to use it or if it would rob us of all the fun of spontaneous sex, but what we discovered delighted us.

We were fine using some self-discipline and we rejoiced at the freedom of using no artificial methods of contraception. We didn't mind abstaining on a few key days a month (if we just couldn't resist, we used a barrier method). The upside of this method is that we learned a lot about how our bodies worked, and we became very aware of when we were feeling amorous, when Pam was fertile, and other bits of information on our sexual organs and systems. We had read a few books on human sexuality while engaged and as newlyweds, but the thorough charting that this method of contraception requires gave us much more insight and information.

As well, we found this method of contraception perfectly reliable. There were no surprises. We can even pinpoint the exact day and time of conception for each of our sons because of this method, and there is something very special about knowing what moment of marital love produced each child.

The other upside of this method is that it trains a couple to use selective abstinence. During the time after birth, or if either partner has an illness or injury that makes sexual relations temporarily impossible, a trust has formed so neither the husband or wife is concerned that a spouse might stray because he or she can't control his/her urges. And that is a wonderful gift of trust!

Another big upside of the Natural Family Planning Method is its affordability. You can purchase a training kit for less than a hundred dollars and it can cover all the years of fertility—or at least until you may want to make a more permanent decision.

Permanent Contraception

Vasectomy (99 percent effective)[15]

The tubes that bring sperm from the testicles to the prostate, called the vas deferens, are clipped in an outpatient surgery. The sexual act remains the same—the husband is just "shooting blanks." The medical community will console you with the information that your male hormone levels, your hair distribution, and your voice pitch will all remain the same.

If, however, you discuss this option with male friends who have had the procedure, they may tell you of small changes in the way sex feels, especially in the first few weeks (or longer) after the procedure. This may be due to the adjustment your body is making due to the surgical procedure. You may also hear stories of times the procedure failed and a baby was conceived, but the actual number of those cases is very minimal.

The usual possibility for failure exists if the man has unprotected intercourse within a few weeks after having the procedure, as some sperm can remain in his semen before it is all flushed out. The doctor should do a recheck a few weeks later to let you know if you are completely sterile and free to have unprotected sex.

A man might want to take a day or so off work, have some bags of frozen peas or ice packs handy, and he'll want his wife to drive him home from the procedure. He can't do any heavy lifting, so at least he gets permission to guiltlessly lie around watching football!

Couples should pray through a permanent choice because even though a vasectomy is reversible, it does mean another surgery, and reversal is not successful in all cases.

Tubal Ligation (approximately 99 percent effective)[16]

In a ligation, a surgeon cuts and cauterizes the fallopian tubes through which the egg travels. Sperm can no longer reach the ovum; the ovum can no longer reach the uterus. It's possible for an ovum to have already traveled down the fallopian tube prior to the surgery, so just in case, a woman should use some form of birth control the first time she has sex after the ligation. It's also possible a woman will enjoy sex a bit less after this procedure for a period of time because, again, it is a surgical procedure. However, many operations are done with a laparoscope now. This is a small scope the surgeon uses to view your insides via a very small incision.

Most women find they enjoy sex more because they are not worried about getting pregnant, and sexual intercourse is not interrupted for a birth control method.

This surgery is a little more expensive than a vasectomy, and some women decide during their last pregnancy they want to have the procedure done at the birth. This might save money but can also be a very emotional decision. Some women elect to have the surgery at a time separate from the birth of their last child, even though the cost might be more. The peace of mind on such a final decision is worth it.

Not Tonight, I Have a Headache

We've mentioned that abstinence is also a very successful form of birth control. We recommend it to married couples only for its temporary use with Natural Family Planning Method, during certain seasons of pregnancy, or right after a baby is born. Be honest: sex is one of the reasons you two got married, so abstaining can put your marriage in danger. If you and your partner are newlyweds and you are not enjoying an active, vibrant sex life, something is definitely wrong. You should seek out medical help or marital counseling immediately. If you or your mate is not feeling in the mood and this lasts more than a few months, do not think it will magically heal itself.

It is very common for women to have certain days when they are more amorous (the body signals its desire for sex on most fertile days), and other days when they have little sexual interest. Women who suffer from PMS will experience bloating, breast tenderness, weight gain, abdominal pain, and other symptoms that can dampen their desire for sexual intimacy. Stress in life (at work, at home, or in the marriage) can also lower their desire for intimacy.

• • •

In the following chapters, we'll give you some ideas on how to fan the flame and keep the spark and sizzle in your sex life. But one key aphrodisiac is to know you have a plan for when or if you want to get pregnant—and when you don't.

The GIFT

Are you happy with the contraception plan you are currently using? Would either of you like to investigate any of the other options listed in this chapter?

Unwrapping the GIFT

This chapter was very clinical, so to counterbalance all the medical jargon, seriousness, and sensitivity of this topic, create a special lovemaking session. Surprise your spouse when he enters the house by cooking dinner in just an apron—or run a bubble bath for two, float some rose petals and light some candles, then leave a trail of paper or confetti hearts from the front door to the bathroom. Plan to be passionately out of control!

12

Baby Makes Three

Do you find yourself wistfully admiring your friend's newest bundle of joy? Are you finding yourselves migrating to the baby department while out shopping? Are your conversations leading to statements like, "When we have kids . . . "? Are you asking your parents, mentors, and friends questions about child raising, or what it was like when a baby entered the equation of their own love lives? Are you purposely walking by maternity stores and looking in the window? If your answer to any of these questions is yes, chances are the baby bug has bitten!

The birth of a child is one of the unforgettable experiences in life. Our first, Brock, was due around Christmas, so we geared up to have a holiday celebration like no other. As the due date approached, Pam's entire family drove down to celebrate the holiday with us since she was in no shape to travel. They all sat around on Christmas day staring at her swollen tummy, waiting for her to go into labor! To everyone's disappointment, Brock stubbornly decided to be a New Year's Eve baby rather than a Christmas baby.

The sense of wonder in my (Bill) heart was unbelievable. As they placed Brock in my arms and congratulated me on my entrance into fatherhood, I remember praying, "God, thank you for this remarkable gift. Help me be the kind of dad this boy needs." I looked at my son and said, "Welcome to life, partner. Together we will figure out whatever it means to be father and son." Then I thought, *This is my son. I will do whatever it takes to provide for this little one, whatever it takes to love this guy, whatever it takes to train him to be who God wants him to be.* In an instant, I saw 1 John 4:18 come alive: "Perfect love drives out fear." The love that rose in my heart for this little guy drove out any fear I had up to that point about being a dad. The cost simply didn't matter anymore because love had taken over.

Some of you reading this book are already parents. Perhaps you got this book as a gift after you'd been married a few years, or it was having a baby that made you acutely aware that you didn't have all the answers or all the skills necessary for having a fulfilling, lifelong love relationship. Or maybe you got the cart before the horse and the baby came before the wedding, so you have a whole new learning curve. For some of you, it is a blended family situation and you are wondering if you should follow the "his/hers/ours" family model and have another child together. No matter where you find yourselves today, your decisions regarding parenting will dramatically change your life.

Prep Time

We believe there is a reason God gives us nine months before the baby arrives. We need that time to prepare our hearts and lives for the responsibility of parenthood! The economic factor is no small consideration: the birth itself plus all the baby paraphernalia can set you back a huge chunk of change. If you have a loving and generous family and friendship circle, a baby shower or two can equip you with the essentials, but you will need to add to your budget the cost of doctor visits, hospital fees, diapers, baby food, and assorted infant care products.

If you take the time to talk with almost any older relative or friend who is a parent, you will probably get the consensus that none of them really felt they could "afford" their first baby (or any of the others that followed!). Some might tell you the timing was less than perfect (early in marriage or during grad school, or before they had a savings nest egg). But they have all survived and had happy, healthy families, so you can see God has a way of adding himself and his miracles to the mix of the parenting process. When he calls you to parenthood, he will equip you for the journey!

When I discovered I was pregnant with Brock, Bill was in seminary and had no job because he was taking more than a full load of courses (almost double that of the average student) so he could get through quicker. We had raised some financial support, our church was giving us some scholarship monies, and I was working full-time and going to school part-time. Early in my pregnancy, some medical issues required that I change to a job that was less physically demanding (and paid a bit less). As he always has, God worked it all out. We did all we physically could do to work and God met us in our efforts and multiplied the money so it became enough.

Parenthood has an amazing ability to make us all work harder and smarter to save better and sacrifice more willingly. Parenthood changes you, so even if you can't see how all the pieces of the puzzle will come together, trust that God has a plan to bring you a future and a hope. Remember he loves that little one even more than you do! It is important to believe in God's provision but not rest on your laurels and presume he will do it all. He will work through you to provide all that your new little one will need. Think and talk through the issues involved so you can prepare as best you can for the opportunity to impact a life for eternity.

The pursuit of parenthood is such a life-changing event that critical questions will arise as you seek God's will in this area of life.

STOP Take a break and begin discussing your hopes and dreams for parenthood. Describe your fears and reasons why you are ready or not ready. The questions we raise in this chapter will make good starting points for discussion. It is impossible to talk about all these issues in one sitting, so when you get tired of exploring this topic, reschedule with one another to pick up the discussion again. Keep this process going until you have covered all the questions to your satisfaction.

Are We Ready?

The first category of questions relates to your readiness to become a parent.

Where Are You Financially?

Do you have a grasp in general of how much adding a baby to your lives will cost? Have you checked your insurance policy regarding maternity benefits before you get pregnant? A good insurance policy might seem expensive each month, but it still may save you thousands of dollars in the end. Are you aware of the range of costs you would incur with your OB/GYN and your local hospital?

How Strong and Stable Is Your Marriage?

Adding a baby into a family system is stressful, so if your marriage is struggling, work on strengthening it first. You could join a small group at church that is studying marriage; attend a marriage enrichment weekend—we offer them, as do Family Life and Marriage Alive; attend an intense marriage retreat like Retrouvaille, Marriage Savers, or Christian Marriage Encounter; do your own weekly Bible study at home using a book on marriage; read a daily devotional for married couples; pray together daily; get a mentor couple; seek counseling if the problems seem too deep to deal with alone.

Have You Had Any Child Care Experience?

If so, what kind? Working in the church nursery? Babysitting while growing up? Caring for friends' or relatives' children? What kind of further experience would you like to gain before having your own child?

Do You Have Training in Basic Child Safety?

Would you know what to do if a child chokes, his heart stops beating, he stops breathing, is bleeding, or breaks a bone? Do you have current information on car seats, cribs, toy regulations, and so forth? Do you know how to baby-proof your home?

Are We on the Same Page?

The second category of questions relates to how you will actually parent the children God gives you:

What Kind of Birthing Experience Do You Want?

Will you deliver at home with a midwife, in a birthing center, in a traditional hospital stay? Will you use Lamaze or other labor-breathing techniques? Will you use any painkillers?

Who Will Care for the Child?

It is our recommendation, and studies back us up, that a child needs to have one of his/her parents as the primary caregiver in his/her earliest years.

Pediatrician T. Berry Brazelton and child psychiatrist Stanley I. Greenspan agree in their recent book *The Irreducible Needs of Children*: "We do not recommend full-time daycare, 30 or more hours of care by non-parents, for infants and toddlers if the parents are able to provide high-quality care themselves and if the parents have reasonable options."[1] A 2000 survey on child care polled both parents and child advocates regarding which care they thought was best during a child's earliest years. Seventy percent of parents and 71 percent of child advocates believed that the best care is an at-home parent.[2]

If You Have to Work, Who Will Care for Your Child?

If, after researching all financial options, you and your spouse both are completely out of the question as daytime caregivers, who would be best? Again, family has a vested interest so, next to you, another relative would be the best option. Other options include a licensed day-care facility and a licensed at-home day care provider like a nanny. If you or your relatives will not be the caregivers, you will want to interview numerous people before you make your decision to insure your convictions will be reinforced. Get references!

Can We Afford Child Care?

If you both have to work, what changes will you need to make, and how can you achieve the financial goals needed to provide the care for the baby after he or she is born?

Have You Talked Through Your Philosophy of Parenthood?

What form of discipline did your parents use with you? Did you think it was effective? What form of discipline would you feel comfortable with using with your own children?

What Resources on Parenting Have You Invested In?

Do you feel you are well educated and equipped? Pam read at least a hundred books when we were considering parenting and expecting.

Who Cared for the Children in the Home You Grew Up In?

Who cooked, bathed the children, rocked them, changed the diapers? What division of labor will you share to care for your own baby? (When you are both home, who will change diapers, feed the baby, bathe the baby, read to the baby, play with the toddler, childproof the house, and so on?)

Will the Baby Be Nursed or Bottle-Fed?

Medical research and sociologists agree that breast-feeding is better for the child than feeding him or her formula in a bottle. Breast-fed babies are better protected from disease and gain other learning and developmental benefits. The medical community recommends that babies are breast-fed the first six months to a year. The La Leche League is a nonprofit organization that provides free information to help mothers who want to nurse become successful at it.

A part of the decision needs to be the honest discussion of how breast-feeding may impact your love life. Many couples find breast-feeding to be a plus to their intimate lives because often a woman feels more shapely and sexy. Men may wonder if they are still free to caress or suck on their wives' breasts. Medically, there is no negative consequence whatsoever, and often women have a heightened orgasmic experience when loved this way. Breast milk is very sweet, so a husband may enjoy its taste.

Still, early in the nursing process a woman's breast may be very tender, so lovemaking that includes the caressing and suckling of the breast might be painful. What is most important is creating the atmosphere where a wife can share what pleases her or what is uncomfortable for her.

Will the Baby Be Fed on a Schedule or Whenever the Baby Is Hungry?

Child-rearing books differ on this issue. So do other moms, but an informal survey of friends can help. We found that with our children we became less rigid with the schedule with every baby we added. This is one you can research ahead of time and adjust once the little one arrives.

Will the Baby Come to Bed with You?

Every couple needs to do their own research on "the family bed" and decide when a child can or cannot sleep with Mom and Dad. Just a note about this: the family bed can be a hard habit to break when the toddler gets older. Plus, if a child is always in bed with you, when will you have sex? As much as you love your child and want to be close to him or her, it is unwise to put a wedge in your marriage relationship over this.

Do You Have a Long Fuse?

Do you know what Shaken Baby Syndrome is? This occurs when a baby is shaken in anger so harshly that that baby suffers physical damage to its body or brain. If you are easily angered or an impatient person, you should address that issue in some personal counseling or anger-management classes before having a baby.

Have You Taken Child Care and Childbirth Classes?

Do you have thorough and realistic knowledge on what to expect from the birth process? From each stage of the child's life?

The Effect on Your Marriage

Preparing well, learning about parenthood together, can be quite an enriching experience for a married couple. Still, parenthood will radically change your marriage dynamic. As Bill shared, I (Pam) experienced medical issues that ultimately required bed rest for the last four weeks of my pregnancy. I had to forego working as well as whittling away at my education at that time. A friend had to do all my Christmas shopping, and Bill had to completely take over the household chores on top of his grad-school classes!

Children will radically change your marriage, in good ways and some inconvenient ways: A baby is hungry, cranky, needs his/her diaper changed at some pretty inconvenient times. The child becomes the priority for both of you. This new life will need to be nurtured, educated, and morally trained. And as he or she gets older, you will find yourself dishing out money for lessons, sports, fashion, camps, weddings, cars—and maybe even a down payment on their first home!

But all of these sacrifices pale in comparison to the thrill, the enjoyment, the fulfillment—the miracle of your sperm and your egg united to create new life: your child, a visible evidence of your love for one another.

The Harder Questions

Some of you will have to deal with another challenge. You may have trouble getting pregnant, or you may discover that pregnancy is not going to happen for you. In those cases, you have a whole other set of questions to ask: *Do we pursue fertility treatments? Do we want to be foster parents? Do we want to adopt? Do we want to forego raising children altogether?*

Fertility Treatments

A couple have to be free from any form of birth control and must have tried to have a baby for at least a year before a doctor will diagnose infertility. When you need help to become parents, you face a whole Pandora's box of ethical and moral questions.

- Is it God's will to ask for medical help or should you just pray and have sex and leave the results to God?

- If you do pursue help, which kind of help is moral? Is it moral to be on a drug that might produce numerous embryos? Is it moral to use methods like in vitro fertilization? If so, should you only use the father's sperm or can a donor (known or unknown) be utilized? Is it moral to freeze fertilized embryos—if so, how long? Is it ever moral to dispose of, sell, or destroy these embryos?

- What about using a surrogate mother? Should the surrogate carry a baby only if the embryo is the product of the mother's egg and father's sperm? What about the sperm of the father and the egg of a surrogate? And what is the moral compensation for the sacrifices required of the surrogate mother?

The issues become very, very complex. We recommend that if you are struggling with any issues of infertility, you do a few things:

1. Ask God to lead you by Scripture and by advice from leaders who know Scripture.

2. Consult a physician and learn the details of every option available to you.

3. Consult an expert in ethics and morality. Many solid Bible teachers and professors have written articles and books dealing with these complicated and highly emotional issues. (Personally, we recommend the apologetics

department of our alumni, Biola University. Writers such as Dr. Scott Rae are leading the way in discussing some of the most difficult issues involved in the area of where science meets the family.)

4. Pray with a committed set of friends, family, and mentors who know God and know you two. Use these people as a sounding board to talk through some of the most difficult issues in your particular case.

Foster Parenting

Many of our friends have begun or expanded their families through becoming foster parents. Rich and Leslie wanted to be parents but were concerned that, because of a medical condition, Leslie would risk her life in a pregnancy. They decided to be foster parents. This involved some extra work on their part: classes, a home study (and the preparations necessary to prepare their home to pass a home study), a background check on everyone in the home, fingerprinting, physicals, and time spent with other foster parents interviewing them on the foster-care system and their personal experiences with it. The process, once a couple decides to become foster parents, can take up to six months or more.

Rich and Leslie knew the need for foster families was great, but it wasn't until they considered the possibility for themselves that they learned how vast the need for quality families really was. More than five hundred thousand children in the United States are living in foster care. Most children go into foster care because they've been neglected or abused or their parents have alcohol or drug addictions. On average, a child who enters foster care will be there about two and a half years. Just 50 percent will return to their parents.[3] Biblically, if you decide your marriage is strong enough to handle the uniqueness of loving foster children, you would be carrying out the call in Psalm 82:3: "Defend the cause of the weak and fatherless; / maintain the rights of the poor and oppressed." Still, God doesn't call every couple to do this.

It is wise to investigate all that being a foster parent, or an adoptive parent of a former foster child, entails. These children are in desperate need of wonderful, safe, healthy homes, but parenting them can be especially intense. Many of these children have suffered traumatic experiences in life.

If your marriage is strong and stable, you may be able to handle the unique challenges of parenting these precious but needy children. But most foster parents are not newbies in parenting. They are parents who have at least one child of their own and have some idea what to expect.

Adoption

About 100 million Americans have adopted kids in their families.[4] The price tag on adopting a child can range from nothing (there is even a stipend given to adopt some children in the foster-care program) to private or international adoptions that can be quite expensive (in the tens of thousands of dollars). This is why many who adopt, especially those who opt for international adoption, are from upper middle class families.

However, some churches and some friendship circles see adoption as a calling or a unique form of missions. This is especially true of adoption of children from countries where they have little chance of survival or little hope to hear the life-saving message of a personal relationship with Jesus. We have had many friends adopt children from overseas and their entire friend, church, and family circles contributed to defray the cost of the adoption.

Adoption is a very biblical concept since we, as believers in Christ, were "adopted": "For he [God] chose us in him before the creation of the world to be holy and blameless in his sight. In love he predestined us to be adopted as his sons through Jesus Christ, in accordance with his pleasure and will" (Eph. 1:4–5). Adoption clearly reflects the heart of God.

Adoption, like all methods of becoming parents, is not without risks. "Although adoptees make up only 2 to 3 percent of the population, statistics consistently indicate that 30 to 40 percent of the children found in special schools, juvenile hall and residential treatment centers are adopted."[5]

The biggest risk in many adoption cases is that of the custodial mother or father changing her or his mind and deciding to keep the baby after agreeing to release a child for adoption. A couple seeking to adopt may go through this experience more than once before a finalized adoption is completed, so adoption is not for the faint of heart. However, you are modeling the heart of God when you adopt, because we all have been adopted by God as children; if you adopt, the God who knows all about adoption will be there for you.

• • •

The bottom line is, if God is laying parenthood on your heart, make sure you are in agreement about the particulars as well as thoroughly prepared. If you already have children, strive to be the best parents God can make you. Children are an enormous blessing, but they require enormous preparation and work! Make all your "baby makes three" decisions with prayer.

The GIFT

Set aside time to discuss all the questions about parenting in this chapter. We used valuable drive time to prepare for parenting. I (Pam) would read aloud from parenting books, and when we came to discussion questions, I'd look up verses and we would dialogue on them. I made notes while Bill drove. There are many great parenting books. Of course, we hope you read ours—*The 10 Best Decisions a Parent Can Make*—but we also appreciate the works of Dr. James Dobson, Kevin Leman, Gary Smalley, John Trent, Jill Savage, Lisa Whelchel, Jim Burns, Dennis Rainey, Brenda Nixon, and Dr. H. Norman Wright. Spend some time sowing research that will reap the investment of a successful family and a strong marriage.

Unwrapping the GIFT

Some couples find it meaningful to make love in a special place when trying to conceive. Is there a place that is special to the two of you: the city where you met, the place you honeymooned, a vacation spot with happy memories?

Other couples find it special to make love in the nursery after conception has taken place because they feel closer to the anticipated baby.

Other couples find it fun to "practice" conceiving. When you are trying to get pregnant, come up with fun ways to invite your mate to make love to you. Send a bootie and a "Please come home at lunch" note in his briefcase or put a yellow rubber duckie on the bathroom sink in the morning with a note on its neck: "See ya tonight for some baby-making practice."

Once you are pregnant, be prepared: your sex life will be like a roller-coaster ride. The first few months a woman may feel extremely tired and not up to sex—or she might have a queasy stomach with morning sickness (or in some cases, *all-day* sickness). In those middle few months, though, testosterone builds up so a woman is often more amorous than usual and her husband may have to work to keep up with her desire to have sex! Enjoy it!

For nearly all couples, sex while pregnant is completely safe for the wife and the baby. Those middle few months may be God's reward for your patient understanding for the early months of pregnancy when a wife might be less than enthusiastic, and for the last few weeks when she is feeling bigger than a barn and uncomfortable so her interest in sex may not be as strong as usual. There is also a time after birth (from a couple of weeks to six, depending on the type of birth) when sexual relations will be off limits, so whenever that wife wants to make love during the pregnancy process, go for it because the mood or the opportunity will not always be there!

The upside of the time when sexual intercourse is either not possible or not desirable on the wife's part is that it is her opportunity to give the gift of sexual gratification to her husband by other means. She can experiment with oral sex or hand stimulation.

One method your husband will appreciate and that will be physically comfortable for the wife is what might be called "making fire." To please your mate in this way, simply take his penis in your hands and gently rub up and down the shaft with the same movement you used to use when making clay coils in second grade, or in the same motion you might use if rubbing sticks together to make a fire. When you approach the head, if you apply gently a little downward pressure you will send him to ecstasy! He will most likely ejaculate fairly quickly, so have a towel on hand. He will have a smile on his face and a grateful heart toward you, and you will discover he is very motivated to please you in all kinds of ways in and outside the bedroom.

If you are a couple struggling to conceive or putting off the decision till later, your GIFT might be an adults-only date. Take a trip to places children rarely go: the symphony, the opera, and then home for some sizzling sex in your favorite room in the house that is NOT the bedroom—sex outside the bedroom is something that will be a very rare occurrence if children do enter your life!

By seeking to please one another all the way from conception through pregnancy, you give the baby a loving home, and you will have a strong marriage filled with many days and nights of rich, satisfying sex—some of which will result in babies, and all of which will result in precious memories and an unbreakable bond.

Part Four

Tough and Tender

The Secret for Long-Lasting Love

13

I Will Be Tough on Me but Tender Toward My Spouse

Over the years, we have heard lots of stories, but one couple's experience illustrates just how weak we can be in our humanity. It involves one of the most creative couples we know. They love spontaneity and often push the edge of the envelope to squeeze the most out of every experience.

They were vacationing in Florida and wanted to stop at the Mall of America in Minnesota on their way back to Canada. The husband drove all night to get to the massive shopping center while his family slept. They played and shopped all day before leaving for home. Since he had been up all night and all day, they decided that his wife would begin driving their full-size van.

The family settled into the van with the husband lying down in a makeshift bed in the back. Forty-five minutes into the trip, she realized that she should have gone to the bathroom before they began. She spotted a sign for a rest stop so she pulled in. She looked back at her family and realized that everyone was still asleep. She left the engine running, slipped out, and used the facilities. When she got back in the van, she looked back to see that everything was okay and headed down the road, proud that she had pulled it off.

Three hours later, her two young kids began to stir and one of them asked, "Mommy, where is Dad?"

She answered, "He is in the back sleeping."

"No he's not."

"What do you mean—he is not there?"

"He is just not there."

She pulled off the road thinking her kids were making a mistake. She dug through the covers of the bed and sure enough, he was missing.

The first thing she did was call her parents, "Hi, Mom and Dad. Have you heard from Bob?"

"No, he is with you."

"Actually, he isn't. I must have left him at the rest stop."

She managed to flag down a patrolman to assist her.

"When was the last time you saw your husband?"

"It was about three hours ago at a rest stop somewhere in Minnesota."

"Your husband has been missing for the last three hours?"

"Yes, but I know he is at a rest stop."

"Which rest stop, ma'am?"

"I don't know."

"Do you know which road the rest stop is on?"

"The one that leaves Minneapolis."

"There are five roads that take you out of the city. Which one was it?"

"I don't know."

Well, it turns out that the rest stops in Minnesota are manned, so together our friend and the patrolman called all the rest stops in the vicinity of Minneapolis. They eventually found the one where her husband was sitting, visiting with the attendant.

"Hi, Bob."

"Ha. Ha. Ha" was the first thing he said to her.

"I am so sorry I left you. I'll come get you."

"No, no, no. You tell me where you are and I will come to you."

Bob encountered a truck driver at the rest stop who was heading in the direction where his wife was stopped. It was a three-hour trip to catch up with her, but fortunately he met an interesting man driving the truck.

Bob had a perfect opportunity to be mad and rake his wife over the coals. Any statements about her being irresponsible or out of touch would be obviously accurate. Instead, he chose to fill in the gaps. He stayed put until he heard from her. He got a ride with a truck driver. He took over driving after he caught up with her.

By the way, lest you think women are the only ones who make mistakes like this, we know another couple who experienced the same thing—except the husband was the culprit!

We all make mistakes. It is what we do in response to the mistake that makes the difference between great marriages and miserable couples.

You Can Count On It!

Mistakes will happen. You will make them and your spouse will make them. Even though you are in love with each other and have intentions to do good to each other, you will be subject to your own inconsistency. As you interact with one another, you will continually discover along with the apostle Paul, "I know that nothing good lives in me, that is, in my sinful nature. For I have the desire to do what is good, but I cannot carry it out. For what I do is not the good I want to do; no, the evil I do not want to do—this I keep on doing" (Rom. 7:18–19). The way you respond to the inconsistencies will determine the quality of the life you share together.

There is a way to make the contradictions in your souls work for you, if you are willing. As Paul continued to talk about this inner wrestling match, he challenged us to make a choice that creates a whole new way of living: "For if you live according to the sinful nature, you will die; but if by the Spirit you put to death the misdeeds of the body, you will live" (Rom. 8:13). So, what does it mean to live "by the Spirit" and "put to death the misdeeds of the body"?

We think the process can be summed up as being tough on yourself and tenderhearted toward your spouse. The natural tendency in our human nature is to be selfish and self-serving. We do what we say we don't want to do and we fail to do what we claim to be the right thing to do. We tend to excuse our behavior while we judge others for not living up to our expectations.

STOP Each couple has "gold medal moments" or times when your spouse handled a mistake you made really well. Tell your mate about one of his or her "gold medal moments." Share with them how you felt as a result of his or her wise behavior.

The Path Less Traveled

Powerful, lasting love does not happen by accident. It is reserved for couples who are willing to venture onto the scarcely traveled path of Ephesians 5. In verse 21, Paul charged couples to "submit to one another out of reverence for Christ." The term used here for "submit" comes from the Greek word *hupotassomenoi,* which means "to line one's self up under, to submit."[1] The word is a military term that refers to an officer who voluntarily ranks himself under another officer to help fulfill the mission. It is a position of great strength to be able to subordinate oneself and it is a position of great influence to give of yourself so that someone you love can succeed.

Paul repeated the command to wives to "submit to your husbands as to the Lord" (v. 22) because a wife's submission helps meet a man's deep need to succeed. A man is drawn to the areas of life in which he senses proficiency and he loses interest in the areas of life in which he feels incapable or inefficient. When a wife chooses to give of herself to help her husband fulfill his dreams and responsibilities, she becomes extremely valuable to him. His motivation increases, his interest in her grows, and his impact on those in his life grows more positive.

When Paul wrote this passage, society considered wives as property to be treated at the discretion of the husbands. When Paul called believers to submit to one another, he proclaimed that men and women were equal in ability, colleagues in ministry, and mutually beneficial in one another's lives. Paul's statement freed women to be loved and respected. Paul challenged men to cherish us as equals, and he challenges all of us to mirror the attitude of Jesus who gave himself for us. Help your man succeed!

Shifting into Selflessness

Paul had a lot more to say to a man who wants to be in love with a woman than he ever said to wives. Husbands are called to love their wives in three different ways: "Husbands, love your wives, just as Christ loved the church and gave himself up for her to make her holy, cleansing her by the washing with water through the word, and to present her to himself as a radiant church, without stain or wrinkle or any other blemish, but holy and blameless" (Eph. 5:25–27).

1. A Husband Is to Sacrificially Love His Wife

Just as Christ gave himself so that the church could have eternal life, a husband is to selflessly give of himself so that his wife can reach her potential. This certainly includes the commitment to die for her, if necessary. Most men would admit that the heroic act of dying for their wives would be easier than the day-to-day sacrifices that make wives feel valued. Listening to them as they share their day, taking care of chores around the house that are out of their skill set, and helping them process their emotional reactions to life are much bigger sacrifices that pay off big.

2. A Husband Is to Give His Wife Secure Attention

Paul used two pictures to get his thoughts across. A loving husband is to do all he can to "make her holy," which means she is set apart for special purposes. This picture comes out of the temple where common, or clay, vessels were used to clean up after the sacrifice was slain but precious metal vessels were set apart to actually carry the blood to the altar. The idea is that your wife is to be set apart in your heart as the most valuable person in your life who engages in the most important activities.

The second picture is that of "cleansing her by the washing with water through the word." "Word" here denotes the spoken word and carries the idea of preparing her for the special purposes she holds in your life through words you speak. These words make her realize the supreme place she holds. In other words, God calls husbands to sincerely, consistently, and abundantly compliment their wives!

3. A Husband Is to Give His Wife Synchronized Affection

The idea here is that a husband ought to take the same care with his wife as he takes with himself. A man who truly loves his wife will "feed" her, which means he will do whatever it takes to bring the nourishment to her that she needs to fully develop. As we've mentioned, a man will also "care" for his wife, which indicates he will carry out his responsibility to her with tender love and affection. In other words, he will work as hard to take care of her as he does to take care of himself.

God knew we needed a system to help us practice this "tough on me, tender on you" concept so he gave us the keys in Ephesians 5. This passage models how a husband ought to be tender and lay his life down for his wife and how a wife can be tender by honoring and respecting her husband. Both are tough calls to maintain but will produce a marriage full of tender moments. The fruit of this kind of tender love will produce some sparks in the bedroom—in a good way!

Love in Those Daily Irritations

There is a very practical scenario in our marriage that reminds us often of the need to be both tough and tender. A month before our wedding, Bill and I went in to our pastor for premarital counseling. On that night he asked, "Pam, what is the one fault of Bill's that drives you crazy?"

I sat silent for a long while. I couldn't really think of any faults Bill had. Finally, almost by default I said, "Well, it is no big deal but he's usually seven minutes late."

The pastor smiled and said, "Well, if you can live with it now you'll be okay—because it'll only get worse." And the pastor was right. I (Bill) have to honestly admit that my natural tendency is to be late. There are times when it is no big deal but there are many situations in which I need to be on time, every time. I have had to be tough on myself to get to work, to begin services and conferences, and to get to important appointments on time.

On the other hand, I (Pam) have had to learn to be compassionate about this tendency in Bill's life. A few years into our marriage I found that I was routinely irritated at him for getting home late. He'd walk in the door and I'd be fuming on the inside. One night I could contain it no longer. I erupted! When he entered the front door a half hour later than he said he would be home, I read Bill the riot act. I went on and on. Then I looked at the clock. An hour had passed. I was angry that I had lost thirty minutes with Bill—and I was angrier that I had lost another hour with my ranting.

It was then that some advice from a doctor's wife I knew rang in my head: "Being married to an obstetrician, I never lose valuable time together complaining that he's not here enough."

That night I chose to forgive Bill—over and over. He's in ministry, and ministry "hours" aren't regular. Bill is a great listener, and people are a priority with him. That is why I fell in love with him. So I have chosen to not expect Bill to make up for the late trait in his life.

The key to long-lasting love is being tough on yourself in your areas of needed growth and tender with your spouse about his or her shortcomings. The first year of our marriage we had lots of opportunities to practice this. When Bill's car died, I (Pam) could have become demanding, irate, and belittling in my conversations with comments like, "Why can't you provide?" or "I should have married a guy in a career, not college" or a host of other hurtful and very unproductive things. Instead, I said, "What can I do to add to our finances so we can work toward replacing this?" I switched to a job with more hours and better pay and benefits.

In the same way, a few years later Bill returned the favor when

I became pregnant with our first child. For the first few months, I was really sick and pretty worthless. Bill could have said, "Come on! Millions of women worldwide have to work when they are pregnant. Buck up, babe!" Instead, he got an extra tutoring job so I could regain my health.

When you reverse this, when you are tough on your spouse and tender with yourself, your mate will grow to resent your self-protecting behavior. He or she will respond by going into self-protection mode. Then you will build walls around your hearts, begin to make independent decisions, and drift apart. One day you will wake up and realize you have nothing in common and no reason to stay together.

If, however, you are tough on yourself and tender with your spouse, your mate will be so amazed at your selfless love and sacrifice that he or she will in turn want to love you back in a selfless, sacrificing way. Year after year, you place precious memory after precious memory in your heart for one another. When tough times hit, or if you inadvertently do something really dumb, your mate will have a treasure chest of kindness stored up toward you.

• • •

Jesus modeled this tough on me, tender on you principle when he went to the cross for our imperfections. Daily we reap the blessing of that love. In the same way, God reminds us in Galatians 6:2 to "carry each other's burdens," which means we make allowances for the imperfections in one another and look for ways to lower our spouses' stress level. It is inconvenient at times to do this, so it will feel tough at times, but it will create a tender love that lasts a lifetime.

 **The GIFT**

When you get aggravated with your spouse, ask, *How can I be tough on me and grow through this to be a stronger, better person or help our marriage become a stronger, more stable re-*

lationship? Also ask, *How can I show compassion, forgiveness, and grace to my mate and his/her choices here?* Then say or do something that shows your mate your tenderness. It is like handing your spouse a Monopoly "Get out of jail free" card. When you give grace like this, then you both move ahead on the board game of love.

 Experiencing the GIFT

Speaking of board games, pick up a few at garage sales: Clue, Monopoly, Life, Chutes and Ladders, Twister, Uno, Parcheesi, chess, or checkers. These simple parlor games can take on a whole new meaning if you move them into the bedroom. Select any game, then make a new rule. The winner gets to ask for a "favor" and your mate will seek to please you to your heart's delight.

14

Get to the Heart of Your Spouse

A woman was arrested for shoplifting and had to go to court. The judge asked her, "So, what did you steal?"

She answered, with an embarrassed tone in her voice, "A jar of peaches."

"How many peaches were in the jar?" the judge wanted to know.

"There were six," was her simple reply.

At that, he pronounced his judgment, "You will have to spend six days in jail."

Almost immediately, her husband stood up and raised his hand. The judge was a little annoyed but asked him why he was on his feet.

The husband replied, "Your honor, she also stole a can of peas."

We are so different; it is easy to let those small idiosyncrasies build up over time, until all you are doing is "counting peas." Instead of tallying up the negatives, the healthiest couples focus on the strengths of each spouse that allow them to encourage each other's hearts.

What Makes Your Mate Tick?

Every one of us was born with an inner drive at the core of who we are. It provides energy for the pursuits in life we consider worthwhile and makes it hard to accept the way our spouses like to do things. It determines the way we like to spend money and makes us irritated when our spouses want to handle money in a different manner. It makes certain romantic activities attractive while it makes others seem silly. It explains why some of the things your spouse does are incredibly attractive to you while other behaviors are annoying. And it orchestrates which issues will present problems for you when you are frustrated.

Are you aware of the inner motivation that runs your mate's heart? If you ignore these motivating factors, your mate can begin to feel stifled, resentful, hurt, betrayed, or unloved. If, however, you can get to the heart of your spouse, it will help you:

- Recognize the real issues. When conflicts arise, you will have better insight into how to resolve them quicker and easier.

- Reward your successes. When your spouse goes the extra mile for you, you will be able to give the kinds of rewards that truly matter to your partner.

- Relax your spouse. You will help lower the overall stress level of your home.

- Run your budget. You can organize your finances around your inner drives so your money plan reflects who you are. As a result, you will have more energy to manage your budget and will feel less insulted by the way your spouse does things.

- Romance your lover. You can choose to do the things that will draw your spouse to you over and over again.

There are four primary inner drives. You are highly influenced by one of these and will find that you are consistently drawn to organize your life around it. At the same time, your spouse is most likely driven by a different motivational impulse. This provides great variety for you as a couple and has the potential to make you much better as a team than you could ever be as an individual. It also provides many opportunities for conflict and disagreement.

Identifying each of your core drives is one of the most important insights you will ever gain. To help you in the process, we will discuss each of these central influences and explore how they impact the way you like to handle finances, the way you like to be romanced, the way you like to be encouraged, and the symptoms that reveal themselves when you are frustrated.

> **STOP** Make a copy of the chart "Get to the Heart of Your Spouse" on page 220 or write in the book. In *The GIFT* section, there are specific questions that will help you complete the chart over the next few days.

Read through each of the following four descriptions. Place a star next to the one you think is closest to your heart motivation, and then put a heart next to the one that sounds most like your mate's. As you interact over the next few weeks, deliberately take notice of how your energy level changes when you get to operate according to your inner drive. Also, practice ways to help your spouse operate according to his or her inner drive and notice what happens.

Inner Drive #1: Authority

If this is you, you are motivated by being in charge of the decisions that affect your life. You like options. If there is a decision to be made, you will want your voice to be heard. You are often a first-born and a natural leader. Having a measure of control over your life is a high priority. You would not be considered a "control freak" because you do not need to be in charge of other people's lives, but you do enjoy being decisive when it involves your life.

To others, you seem naturally confident so they assume decision making is a gift you possess. You enjoy it when people look to you for answers, orders, or direction. You may or may not hold a position as an authority figure, but you tend to rise to the top in any group in which you participate. In your marriage, you have an opinion on most topics in the relationship.

- Inside you is a sign that reads, "Let me be in charge."
- The big "do" for those motivated by authority is to communicate their vision for life. You are naturally decisive

and people will interpret this as pride and manipulation if they do not know how they fit into the big picture.

• The big "don't" for those motivated by authority is to be second in charge. You were born to lead! You can be in a support role for short periods of time but you will function best when you find the pursuit God created you to direct.

• What you long to hear is "Let's do it your way."

A Powerful Approach to Life

Money: For those who are motivated by having authority, money is power. It represents options and opportunity. As a result, they are very active with their money. They spend money on whatever goals they consider worthwhile. They invent a plan and take calculated risks to see that plan become a reality.

They are exciting to be around because they are highly productive, visionary, focused, and fearless. They are hardworking, hard-driving people who have the capacity to handle large budgets and large challenges. With spiritual depth and maturity, they can accomplish much for a family, a marriage, a community, or a church. They have a hard time allowing financial opportunities to slip by, so someone motivated by authority either has a lot of money or is completely broke!

The danger for those motivated by authority is the temptation to become power-hungry workaholics. The pursuit can become so important that people fall off their priority list. Authority-driven folks tell the people in their lives that all this hard work is for them, but the relationships can remain distant because the pursuit of power and wealth is like an aphrodisiac to their souls.

Relaxation and Romance: These people need to make relaxing a priority because they are not good at it by nature! If you are married to this spouse, you can extend his or her life by helping him/her step out of the fast lane for some much needed, well-deserved rest and relaxation. When you plan for these people, remember that they work hard and will want to play hard. These people make a list of goals for their vacation: climb a mountain, win the golf tournament, shop in every store on the island. They also like to recharge in an extravagant way: spa packages, ski packages, Club Med with lots of options to select from are a few favorites.

The key thing to keep in mind is that whatever authority-driven people decide is romantic—is romantic! If visiting every major league ball field for a game is his plan for celebrating his birthday year by year, then doing that for him will be a romantic expression. If she sets her heart on Paris for your anniversary, you will win big romantic points if you can pull it off.

Buying gifts for the authority-driven can be a challenge. They are so decisive that they will buy something as soon as they become aware of the need for it. Your best bet is to ask them to make a list each time you want to reward them with something special.

Keys to Encouragement: Encouragement comes in the form of co-operation, which means they set the plan and you cooperate! They value the times you pitch in and help them succeed at the goal without the "you scratch my back, I'll scratch yours" attitude. You can reward them by doing your part well and with a good attitude. They are wired for making decisions and they feel out of control when they have no say in any decision that impacts their lives. If you make a decision without consulting your spouse first, he or she will feel slighted. On the other hand, anytime you trust your spouse's decision making, you are speaking his or her language.

Issues that surface first in conflict: When this person is disappointed or frustrated, it may show up in angry outbursts, cutting words, aloofness, direct attack, or belittling words. The point is you will *know* immediately when your mate is ticked off because you will be told clearly, loudly, directly, and emphatically.

Your best bet is a direct response. Say something like, "Honey, what just happened here? We were talking and now it appears you are upset. I'd like to hear what changed. Can you tell me what the problem is, as you see it, and what you think we should do with this situation?"

When you need to confront an issue, you will have higher odds of success if you present your concern clearly and leave some decision in your spouse's hands. For example, at one leadership conference, a pastor's wife shared a story of a time she needed to approach her husband to explain that she thought she and the toddlers in the home were not getting the attention they needed. She entered her husband's office and said, "I know you are the pastor of this church but you are also the leader of this family. You have a flock, but I think the Bible is clear that I am the first lamb that should be on your heart. I will never bring this up again, but I will pray that God gives you the wisdom and discernment to shepherd the church and our family well. I trust you to do what is best."

The pastor shared later that he was motivated to change his long work hours to something more conducive to a maintaining a family life because "if my wife confronts me because she wants me to be my best, I am motivated to do it. She didn't just whine and complain to meet her needs. She did it because she knew in the end, this would be a better decision for me and my ministry"—not to mention his family!

Inner Drive #2: Attention

If this is you, you are motivated by being noticed. You function best when you are applauded for your efforts! You are people-oriented and you are comfortable being the life of the party. You thrive with all kinds of attention, both personal and private. You may wonder if it is okay but you especially flourish when an experience is "all about you," because you honestly believe everyone is having a good time.

You are energized by public affirmation, whether it is compliments in front of your boss, friends, or even strangers on the sidewalk. The more public the display of affection and attention, the more loved you feel. You know it is not practical but you would love it if your spouse rented out Yankee Stadium and invited the crowd in for your next anniversary!

Because you feed off attention, you are energized by time with people: parties, social gatherings, church events. If people are there, you want to be there. Unfortunately, you also get bored more easily than the average person. When something is no longer fun, exciting, or entertaining, you get restless and begin looking for the next new adventure.

- Inside you is a sign that reads, "Look at me!"

- The big "do" for those motivated by attention is to find a stage! You were made to be in front of people so you can inspire them. If you do not have a career, hobby, or ministry that puts you in front of a crowd, your family will grow tired of being your audience.

- The big "don't" for those motivated by attention is to settle for an unhealthy way of getting attention. If positive attention cannot be found, these people will accept negative attention. Don't let dramatic outbursts, self-imposed crises, or indecision take the place of inspiring those around you.

- What you long to hear is "You are amazing."

A Popular Approach to Life

Money: These people spend money to make memories. Money is all about people. The heartfelt question that they ask themselves over and over is, *How will my spouse [friends or children] feel when I give him [or her] money or spend money on him [or her]?*

The shortcoming is they like to appear as if they have a lot of money—whether they do or not! They love to pick up the tab, throw the lavish party, dress in the latest fashion, or drive the newest, coolest car. They love to spring for trips, shopping, or a day of recreation. They live with the sense that they can purchase friendships or goodwill. As a result, they are very generous; they will give you the last crumb off the table and the shirts off their own backs.

Your family finances work out more smoothly if this person is given the freedom to work very hard to earn extra money that is set aside as discretionary funds. This is money this person can spend as he or she sees fit to enhance relationships. If, however, you hand-cuff these people too much and take away their ability to "bless" the people they love most, they can develop a dramatic edge and become hard to live with.

The solution to the ever-pressing inner need to spend money to gain fun or friendship is to picture your most important relationships at the point of every purchase. When you are ready to make a financial decision, dream of your spouse's face and ask, *Will this please him or her?* or *How will the person(s) I love most feel about this savings or purchase?*

Relaxation and Romance: These are the easiest spouses to romance because they are hopeless romantics. Flowers, chocolates, diamonds, new clothes—all the traditional stuff works with them! They also love surprises, so even a simple expression (like a dozen roses or a new CD) given unexpectedly will get a lot of mileage romantically. What takes romance over the top is to do something public to express your love: call the radio station and ask for "our song" to be played or throw a surprise party. A sure thing with this person is to listen to all his or her hints (and this person does drop hints!), then tie as many of them as possible together into a wonderful gift or outing.

Relaxation for this person comes in the form of public attention, such as a party or some other once-in-a-lifetime kind of event. Because they love memories and people, they relax with trips to see relatives or attend class reunions. They also love to fly their friends or family to exotic locations to celebrate a big moment in life. They enjoy being indulged, so if you are craving a quieter version of R and R, you can make it just for the two of you if there are plenty of people around to wait on your spouse and make him or her feel like a prince or princess.

Keys to Encouragement: These spouses are motivated to keep giving and loving when they are affirmed with encouraging words. You can win them over again and again by giving gifts of time or tangible personal items that say, "I love who you are and want the world to know it." Words said in public that make these people look good are free but reap a priceless reward to keep these mates encouraged. They love to laugh and have a good time so if you bring entertainment into their world, they see that as an incentive to keep engaged in what is important to you.

Issues that surface first in conflict: You are most likely to get a negative reaction if you have somehow made them feel embarrassed in public. Nothing is worse to a spouse with an inner drive so connected to people. Expect a bit of drama: screaming, crying, exaggerated statements like, "You *never* cared!" or "You *always* say [or do]. . . ." Inside these people-lovers is an inner fear that somehow they might not succeed and that would make them look bad to people. When this trigger is kicked off, their overstated emotions will make it clear to everyone that he or she is not doing well.

Once when I (Pam) was under a stressful work deadline, I overreacted to some small mistake Bill made at home. I began to rant and rave, making large, dramatic gestures with my arms, pacing back and forth in our kitchen and raising my voice. Bill recognized the deeper issue, wrapped his arms around me, and said, "Pam, I love you. I am right here. I am by your side. I am your safety net. I won't let you fall or fail. Just tell me what I can do to make the situation better, and I will do it. It will be okay, baby. It will be okay."

I was amazed at how quickly I calmed down. I apologized for my outburst and together we brainstormed a plan that accomplished the goal, thus lowering my stress level.

When your spouse makes a mistake, you can keep the marriage motivation high if you focus on the relationship rather than the behavior. For example, you might say to your spouse when he or she has overspent, "I love you more than that hundred dollars. You are a great person and even the great ones have a bad day on occasion."

Inner Drive #3: Acceptance

If this is you, you are motivated by R-E-S-P-E-C-T! You do not want to be defined by your productivity, your tasks, your job description—or even by your awards or accomplishments. You want to be accepted for who you are and the value you add to life by your presence. You get along with most everybody because you are so easygoing and friendly. You like to be liked and your strongest core value is peace. As a result, you are a big fan of whatever will bring peace and calm to your world.

These people can be so easygoing it can be hard to get them going, unless you know the secret to their motivation: compliment their character rather than their actions. Once you motivate these folks, they are some of the hardest workers ever—and they are loyal. People matter to these folks so they pride themselves on treating people right. They are usually the behind-the-scenes type who make great vice presidents. They have no need to be the Big Kahuna—they are content and fulfilled giving wings to others' dreams as much as their own. They just want everyone to be happy, get along in a peaceful environment.

If this is you:

- Inside you is a sign that reads, "Love me for who I am, not what I can do."

- The big "do" for those motivated by acceptance is to create a team approach to your life and help others succeed. You will find it easy to buy into the dreams of others and will work hard to help lift them up.

- The big "don't" for those motivated by acceptance is to overreact to lists of tasks that need to be done. You will not like to be defined by what you do so you will tend to think lists are a burden rather than seeing them as an opportunity to serve others.

- What you long to hear is "It's good to be with you."

A Peaceful Approach to Life

Money: These folks purchase peace. The goal is to create as simple a process toward money or resources as possible. When the money is there, they are very cooperative. If finances are tight, they get stubborn because they feel as if a crisis is being created that will disrupt the peace in their lives. At this point, they will either work harder, argue, or dig their heels in to find a path out of the crisis.

If the family is spending less than they are making, this person relaxes. If, however, more is being spent than they earn, this person will grow to resent the spending habits of his family as he begins to feel defined as a paycheck rather than a person.

These spouses have a remarkable ability to simplify things when it comes to money. They remind us that life is not all about money. They are peacemakers and natural mediators, so they are good at problem solving financial issues when they are causing harm in relationships and families.

You will find your marriage is better when you commit to a savings account. As long as there is money in the bank to cover contingencies, your spouse can be at peace. In this environment, you will have freedom to do what you want, whether it is seeking a great adventure or building an active social life. As long as you have a simple way to stay ahead, your spouse will be very cooperative.

Relaxation and Romance: This personality knows how to really relax! Vacation to one motivated by acceptance would likely be a week sitting on the beach, relaxing in a quiet, secluded mountain cabin, or being pampered in a quiet spa. The most relaxing thing to do with this kind of spouse is nothing. Take stuff off the calendar, remove yourself from the guided tour list, and just get ready to kick back with your spouse.

The nice part of people motivated by acceptance is that they are so flexible. They actually may not care at all what you do on vacation, or for an anniversary, as long as everyone gets along. If they are in a peaceful environment, they are up for most anything. If you ask your spouse, "What do you want to do for our vacation or anniversary or for your birthday?" be prepared for the response, "I don't know," "I don't care," or "Whatever you'd like to do." Don't take this as apathy. Your spouse really cares for you but doesn't care so much about what you two are doing as long as it is peaceful, calming, and connecting.

Buying gifts for these folks can be a challenge because their personal needs are so small. They don't give hints much and even if you ask them you might get an "Oh, I don't need anything." They are so giving that a good idea might be something personalized or monogrammed so it is for only their use—they can't give it away!

To motivate these spouses, make your gifts all about helping them feel accepted and valued for who they are. Write a tribute that you read to them privately, then slip into their desk drawer. Get a picture or art object that symbolizes their worth and value in your eyes. For example, you may get a statue of an eagle for his office with a note, "Your love has lifted me to the heights and I soar with the eagles because of all you are in my life." Think of creative ways to send cards, e-mails, gifts, or activities that say, "I see who you are and I love it!"

Keys to Encouragement: This person spells love T-I-M-E. As a result, you can keep these spouses encouraged by planning time to just be together with no plan, no purpose other than relaxing and enjoying one another. While spending time together, compliment your spouse's inner beauty and worth. An important step for keeping this spouse engaged in the decision-making process is to respect when you two have put him/her in charge. When a couple decides the acceptance person is in charge of something, it is vital that this responsibility does not get hijacked away. The more decisive spouse makes a huge investment in the future by letting the peaceful spouse hold authority in a few areas.

Issues that surface first in conflict: When spouses driven by acceptance feel devalued, they will get quiet, aloof, distant, pensive, and unresponsive. They also get offended when you embarrass them because they like life to be very private. If you take their lives public without permission, they feel hurt. The world is not right for them. This person has private and public categories of life—do not confuse them! If they are continually hurt, these spouses will withdraw even more and become increasingly unresponsive. At its worst, it is as if they have a magic mute button while you are screaming at them. They just refuse to hear you when they have been wounded time and time again.

I, Bill, am wired this way. Pam made some wise choices early in our relationship that made me feel very valued and set an incredibly positive tone for our marriage. When my car broke down, her willingness to ride her bike everywhere so I could stay in college screamed to my heart, "Bill, you are amazingly valuable!" When she was willing to work jobs that were less than glamorous so I could attend seminary, I felt appreciated. When it was Pam's turn to complete her degree, I was very willing to do whatever it took to help her finish.

The biggest hurdle we had to get over in our early marriage came because of the mixture in my (Pam's) inner drive between attention and authority. When I am under stress, my authoritative need for choices, control, and power kicks in. It isn't always the easiest trait to be around for Bill because I can get pretty bossy. Giving out mandates like "Bill, you should do this" or "You need to . . ." comes easily at these times.

Bill knew he couldn't go our entire married life living under gestapo-like rule, so one day he sat me down and said, "Honey, I know you love me. I know you want me to perform at my peak and do my best, but there are some ways that you talk to me, some phrases you use, that really hurt my feelings."

I (Bill) was relieved when Pam responded with genuine concern, "What do you mean?"

I then gave her some examples and she replied, "You're kidding, right?" She just couldn't conceive how those phrases were hurtful. I explained that she sounded as if she thought I was incapable of figuring out my life on my own. I was starting to feel mothered rather than loved as a husband.

Pam's response was, "Okay, I am not wired that way, but I don't want to hurt you. Teach me how to talk to you in a way I can get my point across but not hurt your feelings. Teach me new phrases to use, new things to say."

So I did. I gave her new phrases to use that did not include the words "should," "just," or "need." To her credit, she practiced using them. I could tell it was hard work for her to change, and it spoke volumes to my heart that she would work so hard not to hurt me. Her sacrifice of love made me feel appreciated, so my motivation to work hard for her, for us, and for our marriage was extremely high.

Inner Drive #4: Accuracy

If this is you, you are motivated by follow-through. You live by the motto: "Do what you said you would do!" If someone says, "I'll be home at six o'clock for dinner" and he or she arrives at six fifteen, you won't consider that person late—you will feel lied to! This happens because you take what others say literally. Promises matter to you.

The details of life stick out because you have been gifted with the ability to see life at a different level than the rest of us. You love long, deep discussions and heart-to-heart talks about life's complex topics. All of this puts you in league with great musicians, artists, computer programmers, and accountants, because nuances matter to them too.

Life will work best for you when it has structure and order. You function well with plans and procedures. Security comes from knowing and working the plan. The plan does not have to be your plan, as it does with the authority personality. You are okay working another person's plan as long as everyone sticks to it as promised!

You have a remarkable ability to be aware of details, so you tend to collect evidence about life. You travel through life collecting data to prove life is either very good—or very bad. Because of this you may be melancholy in personality and prone to depression. When you are collecting positive evidence about life, you have the ability to conclude that life is getting better and better. Unfortunately, you are more likely to collect negative evidence and conclude that life is getting harder and harder. You can spiral downward unless you create a way to interrupt the process.

One of the primary tasks for you in life is to create a bottom to the spiral. This bottom consists of a behavior you choose that keeps your heart from despair. It may be a song you play or a friend you call. It may be a simple activity such as taking a walk, taking a bath, or taking time to read a previously written prayer out loud. The behavior itself is not as important as the fact that you have chosen it and that you do the same thing every time.

- Inside you is a sign that reads, "Pay attention to the details of my life."

- The big "do" for those motivated by accuracy is to prioritize the issues of life and give them only the kind of attention they deserve—since you are prone to treating everything in life as if it is just as important as everything else.

- The big "don't" for those motivated by accuracy is to interpret other people's lack of precision as a personal insult. Their inattention to details is probably not a statement of how they feel about you.

- What you long to hear is "We will stick to the plan."

A Precise Approach to Life

Money: These people are all about a system and they are emotionally attached to the process. When a budget is set, they take the budget literally. So if the budget says fifty dollars for groceries per week, they mean fifty dollars—not fifty-five dollars and not sixty. The budget is a mandate they live by. Still, because they love managing money and resources, they often have money and resources to manage! They are savers, planners, and investors (as long as the investment is prudent and safe).

They spend money according to cautious, practical, and wise long-range planning. This is the spouse that may say "I love you" with snow tires because you need them and tires will keep you safe.

Because they are so inflexible and rigid about the plan, they can often miss great financial opportunities. These spouses will make sure you are never without funding for your life, but cooperating with the budgeting plan might be a challenge for your own personality. The key to working things out is to discuss ahead of time any foreseen changes or adaptations that might need to occur. Accuracy-motivated people are precise but they are generally reasonable, so if you give good reasons, you will get cooperation.

These people need consistent encouragement, so daily expressions of appreciation go a long way in keeping the cooperation level high in your marriage—and helping them stay positive and open to financial ideas you might express. Say "thank you" often and that will help. This should be easy to do if you remember that because your mate is motivated this way, it is highly unlikely you will ever be in a financial bind.

Relaxation and Romance: There is a young couple for whom Bill performed a wedding. At the rehearsal dinner, the groom presented his new bride with a thick scrapbook. In that book were pictures, menus, torn ticket stubs, etc., he had saved from every date they had ever gone on. He also wrote a detailed description of how he felt about her after each date. This couple dated for seven years before they said "I do"! That was one fat album! We think he is still reaping the positive results of that precious, detailed gift to this day!

For relaxation, accuracy-driven people love the deep and meaningful: guided tours with schedules and predictable itineraries, historical landmarks, cultural epicenters like Paris and Rome. These folks might also relax by taking in lectures and conferences to add depth, dialogue, or discussion of the complexities of life.

Romance to these spouses is keeping a promise and remember-
ing significant details about their lives. Don't make promises unless
you are totally committed to follow through. If you want to enhance
the promise, add significant details to it. If you promise to take
your spouse to Hawaii, do so, but put the invitation in a gift set of
their favorite author's books that have been personally autographed.
You will impress them immensely if you can find a first-run, signed
print to hang on the wall to commemorate your time together on
the island. Write a poem recounting this person's sacrifices for you
over the years. Frame it and present it on your anniversary.

Keys to Encouragement: The best way to keep your mate rewarded
is with consistency. Make a habit of sticking to your commitments.
Create regularly scheduled time for deep, detailed conversations. It is
usually enough to tell your spouse that you have set time aside to talk
and then just sincerely ask, "How are you doing?"

Give consistent (daily) compliments, especially in the area you
are hoping to see change in. For example, if he or she is flexible at
all for you, say, "Thank you so much for giving the gift of doing this
the way I needed it done this time. I sure appreciate your flexing
with me."

A huge gift will be to clearly identify decisions so he or she knows
if a particular conversation is just a brainstorming session, a discussion, or making a clear commitment. Discussions often sound like
decisions to this person. As a result, this spouse will begin to move
forward with the plan only to find out it was never really a plan in
your mind. This creates confusion within your spouse and the sense
that your conversations cannot be trusted. It will help you to clearly
delineate for your mate each time you talk by saying, "Thanks for
discussing this with me. Let's brainstorm again before we move on
this, okay?" or "I think we are ready to move on this. Feel free to go
forward with the plan we came up with."

Issues that surface first in conflict: When you do something that
hurts, it wounds the inner core of these people. You can expect these

spouses to become introspective and overanalyze just about everything involved in the situation. They will replay the words and actions over and over again. They might also retaliate by pointing out a litany of your mistakes and shortcomings so they don't feel so bad. Those motivated by accuracy seem to withhold the benefit of the doubt and can become suspicious, accusing, and doubtful of your choices or character.

A simple apology doesn't work with these folks the way it does for most others. This mate will most likely react to an apology with: "So is that all I am going to get? Years and years of 'I am sorry?'" Be prepared to offer new actions that demonstrate your remorse along with some clear accountability. If you get ahead of the game and voluntarily offer a plan for follow-through and accountability, your credibility will rise.

For example, if you have consistently spent over budget, say something like, "Yeah, that is a pretty big fiscal mistake. I am not sure I would trust me either. Here's my credit card. Can you hold it for me for a few weeks so I can learn some new ways to manage my side of the resources?" Whatever your plan is, be ready to live it out because your mate will take your idea literally.

One wife who was motivated by accuracy had a very busy husband intent on climbing the corporate ladder. He would often promise to come home at a certain time so she'd dutifully make a nice dinner only to have him arrive thirty or more minutes late. More often than not, he'd even forget to call and tell her he was running late. He apologized but then would do it over and over again.

Things got so bad that a huge wall developed between them and she was threatening to divorce him because she felt she couldn't trust his word on anything. They ended up coming to us for counsel, and we helped him see that his tardiness was making her feel disrespected and devalued. We worked with her to learn ways of becoming a little more forgiving and flexible and we worked with him on developing romance routines she could always count on to rebuild credibility in her eyes.

Every Tuesday they went to breakfast. Every Thursday was date night. Every day he prayed for her before he left for work and each night he held her and prayed as they dozed off to sleep. The romantic routines reestablished trust in their relationship. Over time, they raised her motivation level so that she asked him for ways she could help him be more successful at work.

To stay in love for a lifetime, you'll be in an endless cycle of give and take. When accuracy-motivated mates crawl out of their comfort zone to do something special for you or to build into your life, thank them in a way they can best hear and receive it. Reward these spouses the way they want to be rewarded—not the way you want to give the reward or the way you would want to be rewarded. By rewarding behaviors, choices, verbal comments they make in a way they like best, you will keep their motivation high—and they will be motivated to keep trying to please you and build into your marriage.

• • •

Proverbs 22:6 says, "Train a child in the way he should go." The term "way he should go" means according to his God-given bent. Each person has a certain bent, an inner motivation that propels him or her forward in life and love. Hebrews 10:24 states, "And let us consider how we may spur one another on toward love and good deeds." In other words, we are supposed to figure out how to motivate one another. The most effective way to influence the energy level of your spouse is to tap into his or her God-given bent.

 The GIFT

This gift is five days long so you have time to observe what keeps your motivation up and what motivates your mate.

Day 1: Try to decide which inner drive best fits you. Are you motivated by authority, attention, acceptance, or accuracy? Now ask the same question about your mate. Write your names in the quadrants on the "Get to the Heart of Your Spouse" chart that best describes each of you.

Day 2: Which money and resource motive most resembles you? Ask your mate if the way you handle money and resources matches the inner motivation you marked. (Note: It should, so if it doesn't, continue this process and you might see a pattern on what his/her inner motivation might be.) Now discuss what changes or adjustments you can make as a couple to keep in mind your money motivations. Write these down on line 2.

For example, because Pam is motivated by attention and making memories with her friends and family is a priority, we created a budget that included an encouragement fund that she has discretion over. Also, early in our marriage when money was extremely tight, we went to a system of cash in envelopes to manage the limited funds. When money was out—it was out. This kept undue pressure off Bill so he could focus on his studies.

Day 3: Share with your mate ideas on what lowers your stress, what you like to do on vacations, and what he or she does for you that makes you feel loved. What has been the most meaningful gift he or she has given you? In the space on line 3, write ideas your mate gives you on his or her favorite way to relax and be romanced.

Day 4: Interview your mate. Write down on line 4 what you can do to reward or thank your mate when he or she tries to help or motivate you. Also write down ideas on what keeps your mate encouraged, motivated, and productive.

Day 5: Ask your mate to tell you what he or she usually does when you have upset him or her. Write that on line 5. Then ask him or her what you have done in the past that helps solve the conflict or repair the hurt. Brainstorm together other helpful ideas on what will calm the rough waters of conflict and remotivate each of you and write the best ideas on line 5.

 ## Unwrapping the GIFT

Enjoy the gift of romancing your mate to motivate him or her. Look at the "what's romantic" list your mate made and create an evening to remember that matches his/her approach to life. Try even to give a sexual gift that complements your mate's motivation.

Get to the Heart of Your Spouse

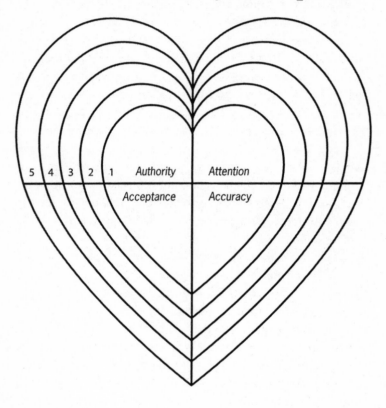

15

Make Conflict Constructive

One man has discovered a creative conflict resolution plan:

> When I go to a local discount store to get oil and filters for my car, I buy my wife a bouquet of flowers from the display near the checkout counter. During one trip, some women in line behind me were oohing and aahing about a husband getting flowers for his wife. "How often do you do that?" one asked. Before I could answer, the cashier, more than familiar with my routine, said, "Every three months or three thousand miles, whichever comes first."[1]

Believe it or not, conflict is one of your best friends as a newly married couple. Arguments provide these benefits:

- They reveal the messages you carry in your heart that are counterproductive to your personal growth and influence.
- They reveal the reasons you fell in love with each other.
- They remind you of the value of your relationship.
- They reveal the personal factors that motivate you.

Let's look at each of these more closely.

The Ways Conflict Helps

Conflicts Reveal Damaging Self-Talk

When you came into the world, you were preprogrammed to believe everything your parents told you. These were the people who loved you the most when you were growing through your most impressionable years. The problem is that your parents were less than perfect, so at least some of the messages they planted in you were negative. Some of us, to be sure, have more of these negative messages than others, but everyone carries a collection of counterproductive messages in his or her heart.

I've (Bill) mentioned that in my childhood years, I was exposed to a variety of messages from parents who loved me very much. I heard, "You are special. We love you. You are smart." At the same time, I heard, "You don't have what it takes. You will never really succeed. You cannot even keep your room clean, and you think you are going to do something great in life?"

For me, these messages had a mixture of consequences. I was confident and willing to step out in new ventures but I didn't know how to finish. The belief that I didn't have what it took to succeed caused me to pull up short in most ventures during the early adult years. For example, I believed I could love Pam the way she was designed to be loved, but I reacted strongly to a couple of phrases she had a habit of using. I mentioned some of these in the last chapter, but the first phrase was, "You remember?" Right in the middle of a perfectly good conversation, Pam would blurt out, "You remember the first time we went to Dewar's ice cream shop, don't you?"

"No, I don't think I do."

"Yes, you do. It was a great day for us," Pam would say as she pursued the agreement that would make her day complete. Then she would leverage the conversation by whining the words that had the ability to pierce my heart: "You rememmberrrrr!"

Two simple words that made my skin crawl. What Pam was saying was, "I want you to remember this because it was such a great memory." What I heard was, "See, you can't even remember a simple detail in your life. I told you, you don't have what it takes. How are you going to pursue a worthwhile career when you can't even remember a day of ice cream?"

The other phrase was, "Bill, just do. . . ." She had a habit of giving advice that began with the word "just" when I brought up a struggle in my life: "Just talk to your boss." "Just hire someone to do it." "Just make the phone call." "Just pay the bills in order of priority." "Just. . . ." "Just. . . ." "Just. . . ."

What Pam was saying was, "You are putting more stress on yourself than necessary. You are the most talented person I know, so I know you can conquer this if you approach it with confidence." What I was hearing was, "You don't get it. You couldn't figure things out as a kid and now you can't figure things as an adult. I am not even sure why I married you, since you can't even get this right."

I (Pam) was hearing a similar mixture of messages. My daddy loved me as much as any dad ever loved his daughter but his alcoholism caused him to be distant and demanding when he was drinking. At times, I heard that I was a princess with a dad who was proud of her. At other times, I heard that I was stupid and could never do enough to get Dad's approval.

As a result, I had some pretty dramatic reactions to things Bill did. During our first year of marriage, we were sitting in our living room enjoying a relaxing evening. We were talking about our childhood years, reminiscing about the good and the bad. In the midst of the conversation, Bill mentioned, "It helps me when the kitchen is clean because it makes me feel like things are under control."

I erupted on him: "You don't love me anymore." With that melodramatic reaction, I ran to our bedroom, slammed the door, threw myself on the bed, and began to sob uncontrollably. Bill followed me into the room and did his best to reassure me that he didn't mean anything by the kitchen comment. It took a lot longer than either of us anticipated to calm my heart down and to reconnect with one another.

Looking back, I realize that what Bill was saying was, "I grew up in a home with unpredictable reactions and unreliable routines. One thing that keeps my emotions calm is a kitchen that is clean. I don't really care who cleans the kitchen, I just do better when it is in order."

What I heard was, "Here is another stupid thing you have done. You can't get the kitchen right and I am sure you can't do anything else right either. You act as if you have things together, but in reality, you are just stupid."

Neither Bill nor I were aware of how intense these reactions were because we had not seen them in any of our dating relationships. They hadn't surfaced in any of our friendships and they certainly had not shown up in any of our ministry relationships. We have since learned that these messages lie dormant outside of intimate relationships. The messages were formed in childhood as we interacted with our parents—the people who loved us the most back then. As adults, we find these messages are triggered by our spouses—the people who now love us the most.

These insecurities and negative emotional reactions became so obvious through these inadvertent conflicts that we had to deal with them. We were either going to get them under our control or they were going to create a huge wedge between us.

Conflicts Remind You of the Value of Your Relationship

In one of your arguments, you will suddenly realize that you do not interact with any one else with this kind of passion, emotion, and need. With others, you have the ability to be objective, rational, and composed most of the time. With each other, you laugh harder, react more strongly, feel deeper, cry more often, and get hurt more easily. No one else can warm your heart or set you on your ear as quickly or as intensely as the love of your life. When it dawns on you that there is no other relationship on earth like this one, you will conclude your spouse is a valuable treasure worth pursuing and protecting.

Conflict Brings Opportunity to Grow Stronger

Intense conflict and ongoing frustration are signals that you as a couple need to learn new skills. This then gives you an opportunity to enhance and fortify your relationship. Still, because new skills are needed, you should seek outside help: a marriage seminar, a weekend conference, small-group therapy, or couples counseling by trained clergy or a professional marriage and family therapist.

So how do you know when you need to call for help?

Call in a counselor:

- If you are feeling physically unsafe. (Get out to a safe place, then call a counselor.)
- If you are feeling verbally assaulted or emotionally betrayed.
- If you seem to fight over and over about the same issue and can't get anyplace trying to talk it out.
- If you are feeling you want out or are tempted to cheat.
- If you have a big decision to make and the conversations are getting emotionally charged.
- You feel you need to learn some new tools to move your relationship forward.
- If you are sexually disinterested for a prolonged period of time.
- If you are disagreeing on a very personal issue (such as sex, child rearing, past baggage, the "ex") and you need a third party to help you two navigate a difficult conversation.
- If one of you is caught in a sin and needs help to get out of a negative habit (such as an addiction to porn, deviant sexual choices, drugs, drinking, gambling, or shopping).
- If you are doing well and want to keep it that way—you want to get a yearly "checkup."

What to do personally if you feel your marriage is in trouble:

- Seek out other couples, mentors, and friends who believe in marriage.

- Do not hang out with disgruntled single friends who resent the institution of marriage.

- Turn up the truth. Read the Bible, listen to praise music, listen to Christian radio, podcasts, or CDs of sermons.

- Surround yourself with people who love you, love your spouse, and love God: join a small group studying marriage (if your mate won't go, join a men's or women's group learning about marriage); go to prayer meetings, worship services, concerts, conferences, and retreats—anyplace you can stockpile the truth in your heart and mind. If you go together—all the better!

- Pray together out loud every day, even if it is only "Lord, we are in need of a miracle from you. Please heal our marriage, and start your work with me." Bill and I have never seen a couple divorce who will humbly get on their knees, hold hands, and pray this simple but profound prayer daily until they experience the miracle of falling in love again! God will meet you two—even in your pain and imperfections. Just ask!

- Seek a counselor early. Don't wait. If you feel you need some outside help, trust your instincts. If your spouse won't go, go yourself. New tools can bring new hope and new life to a relationship.

- Do nice things even if you don't feel like it! Act as if you are in love and you'll be surprised how soon the feeling of being in love will reappear!

- Keep confidences. The best help will be a trained clergy or marriage and family counselors who have to keep things confidential.

- When talking to friends and family about your spouse, use words that honor your mate even if he or she is living in a dishonorable way. Make all statements truthful, but not detailed. Express faith in a good outcome. For example, if asked by friends or family, "Is everything okay with you two?" answer something like:

"We're going through a tough transition right now, but I know God will help us figure it out."

"We're in one of those rough patches, but we are seeking help so I know we'll find the answer."

"Thanks for your concern. Yes, things are a little stressed, so keep us in your prayers."

Family and friends can be of great help to a newly married couple, but carefully select those you confide in and make sure they are people who may have a helpful solution, can keep a confidence, and will not hold errors against you or your mate afterwards. It is best to first agree on getting outside help and choosing whom to confide in. But if your mate refuses to address the issue, you will have to make the choice to get help no matter how he or she feels.

Be tough on yourself at this point! If you are having trouble figuring out the steps of growth by yourself, get help. Find a trusted pastor or Christian counselor and set a game plan for your personal growth. The investment you make now will pay off big throughout the rest of your marriage.

Make Arguments Your Ally

If, however, your conflicts are the garden-variety type—ones you know you can settle between yourselves—there are a few decisions that will make your arguments an ally.

Decision #1: We Will Finish Every Argument

We will keep the discussion going until we have discovered the real source of the argument. Few, if any, couples have the ability to say what the real issue is right up front. Generally, the argument starts over an emotional reaction. In this state of heightened emotional turmoil, it is unrealistic to think that you are going to calmly, succinctly, and skillfully roll out your side of the argument. You will be much more successful if you take time to listen first.

Decision #2: We Will Deal with the Real Issues

Since so many emotional scars from the past come up in arguments, it is not wise to guess what the other person meant or had intended. Often God will use your arguments to expose these messages so you can replace them with healthy messages. Instead of placing your guess at his or her motive on to the situation, ask, "Please explain to me what your thought process was on this."

Decision #3: We Will Get to the Truth

The place to start is with the statement: "Let's identify what God says about each of us that combats the negative messages we heard in our hearts as children that escalated this conflict." Without these messages, whatever conflict you were in would probably have been manageable. Some things you might say to one another: "I know your dad told you were stupid, but that is not what God says about you. He says you have the mind of Christ. He says he will supply all your needs according to his riches in glory. He says he will give you wisdom if you just ask for it."

STOP On a sheet of paper, write down the thoughts and feelings you experienced during a recent argument. Along with each statement, write down a Scripture that declares what God says about you. Refer to it often to help you counteract these negative messages.

Here is an example:

What I thought/felt about myself when we were arguing:

Bill: My first reaction was frustration. I thought, *We speak different languages. I don't think I know how to say what I need to say in a way she will understand. This feels the same as when I was growing up and my mom would refuse to listen to me. It is probably a waste of my time to even talk about this.* My second reaction was determination. I thought, *I know Pam loves me even though the emotions are negative right now. Maybe I can break through all this.*

What God says about me:

Philippians 4:13—"I can do everything through him who gives me strength."

Romans 8:37—"In all these things we are more than conquerors through him who loved us."

Decision #4: We Will Harness All That Emotional Energy

Intimate relationships need both compassion and energy in order to grow and thrive. If you are like most couples, you will not always have both. When a relationship has compassion but no energy, it is a nice but boring place to hang out. You know that your spouse cares about you but there is nothing interesting going on. Your conversations are gentle and kind, but you feel no sense of adventure or romance or purpose. It is fine for a while, but most people want more than that.

When a relationship has energy without compassion, it becomes harsh. Couples make demands and try to manipulate each other. The relationship is exciting and productive, but it lacks an atmosphere that fosters intimacy. Over time, your hearts get bruised and sparks that ignite love disappear. You move from irritation to disappointment to disillusionment. You will probably have the energy to hang in there for a while, but the energy will dismantle your joy.

When an argument breaks out, it is good news because it means there is plenty of energy in the relationship to work with! It probably also means, however, that your compassion for one another has gone temporarily dormant. If you have argument after argument and do not rediscover your compassion for one another, your hopes and dreams will be slowly eroded. It will not be like a car accident that happens quickly and without warning; it will be more as if you are working against each other on a jigsaw puzzle. Every piece you put in place is countered with a move that takes the puzzle apart. Eventually, you just get tired of working on the puzzle and wonder where the joy of being in love went.

Don't let this be your story. Instead, practice merging energy with compassion. Say to yourself, *I wonder how long it will take for us to discover just how good our relationship can be in the midst of this disagreement.* Learn to start arguments with the phrase: "There is something I love about you that is driving me crazy. Will you help me figure out what it is?" When you are engaged in an intense interaction and you can't finish because of other commitments or exhaustion, reschedule the discussion.

This is why Ephesians 4:26 states, "'In your anger do not sin': Do not let the sun go down while you are still angry." It is ideal if you are able to get to the place where you passionately love one another before you go to bed, but it is not always possible in the press of life. Therefore, it is sometimes necessary to put the discussion on hold, but it should never be out of your control.

When you decide to pick it up again at an assigned time, you become the master of the anger and can direct it to work with you rather than against you. If you reach the point where the compassion returns, it mingles with the energy and passion will ignite. Your concern for each other will be intense and the sex that follows will be exciting and memorable.

You have probably heard this referred to as "makeup sex." Sexual arousal is often strong after an argument because there is an intense reminder of the foundation of your passion. As the anger subsides, you remember why you fell in love and sexual energy gets released.

Decision #5: We Will Decide on a Course of Action

When turmoil arises in your life, there may be nothing you can do, or there may be an obvious solution. We know lots of young couples who have to deal with situations that have no real solution.

At other times, there is a solution you can discover and implement. You may have been arguing over financial decisions, but there is one approach on which you both can agree. You may have been disagreeing about how much time to spend with family at the holidays, but you both can tell a solution is apparent.

In order to reach an agreement that does not compromise your convictions, your emotional connection, or the health of your sex life, follow this simple formula of Know, Feel, and Do.

Know. Describe what you know about the situation. Stick to the facts and avoid "you" statements as much as possible. It is better to say, "I am aware that we ran short of money this month" rather than "You spent too much money again." "You" almost always makes the one you love defensive, triggers negative messages from the past, and causes the conversation to be lost before it ever really begins.

Describe how the situation makes each of you *feel.* "When we run short of money, I get scared and I feel as if I have failed in my life. It reminds me of when I was eight and my dad told me I was stupid when it came to money. He said he prayed I would marry someone who was really good with money because if it was up to me, I would probably be broke."

Brainstorm ideas about what you each can *do* to resolve the conflict. Each of you write a list of ideas. Don't judge or evaluate, just list as many ideas as you two can think of. Then evaluate each option. It might sound like this:

"It seems to me we could take the Crown Financial course at church, or we could work through the budgeting plan in *Master Your Money* by Ron Blue. What do you think?"

"I believe it would be best to take the course at church. I am not convinced we have the willpower to do this on our own. I would love to see us make ourselves accountable so that we actually finish the process of figuring out how to be on the same page with money. If friends of ours came to us and asked, I would encourage them to take the course. What do you think?"

"Well, I would rather say that we can do this on our own. I am nervous about letting other people know what is happening in our lives, especially when it comes to our money. I think you are probably right, however. It would be easy to encourage others to take the class. It is a lot harder to decide to do it ourselves, but I think our relationship needs us to do this."

Decision #6: We Will Support Each Other Even if We Cannot "Fix" the Issue

The next step is to ask the question, *Is this one of those situations that we have to adjust to because we cannot fix it?* Examples of situations that cannot be "fixed" include a physical handicap one or both of you has, tension with a relative who refuses to work on the relationship, a special-needs child, the need for more training on the job. At times like these, all you have is each other. No slick answer or ingenious scheme will replace love in the equation. There are a few questions you can ask to help you determine if the situation you are facing is one of these:

- Is this situation caused by a physical trait that is beyond our control?
- Do we possess decision-making authority in this situation?
- Do we have the resources to make a difference in this situation?
- Have we faced a situation like this before and discovered that it did not have a solution?
- Would we encourage our best friends to look for a solution or simply find a way to adjust?

If you conclude the current situation does not have a resolution, give thanks to God that he is committed to walk through this with you and give thanks that you have a spouse so you don't have to struggle with this alone (1 Thess. 5:18). Then ask yourselves, *What can we do to grow in the midst of this challenge since this is going to require us to be at our best?* If you conclude this is one of those situations, end your conversation with prayer that includes a commitment to hang together.

> Lord, we would be lying if we said we are glad for this situation, but we trust you. Thank you that you are committed to help us and that you have given us each other for this journey. Please go before us and prepare us for what this will mean to our lives. Please go with us and give us strength that is beyond our own. Please come behind us and work in ways that only you can to somehow change this situation into something better than it is today. We are committed to each other and we are committed to seeking you in the midst of this. Please do what will bring you the most honor.

• • •

Our choices create our love. When conflict is intense, when you feel pressed into a corner without an answer, consider which decision in this chapter might build a bridge to the heart of your spouse. Your decision could be the Golden Gate bridge over the troubled water into the promised land of lasting love.

The GIFT

Once you have decided how to resolve your conflict, write down your decision. It has been often said, "The faintest of ink is better than the best of memory." So buy a gift for your future love: get a white board or chalkboard for your home. When you make an agreement, write it down in code to remind both of you what you agreed on.

For example: If you agreed not to spend more than one hundred dollars unless you talk about it first, then write the number one hundred with a heart around it on the board. You'll be able to write several agreements in code down before the board is filled up. As you practice the agreements, they will become habits, then you can erase the board to make room for new agreements.

It is valuable to write these things down. You do not want to have another argument later on about what you both remember or don't remember about the agreement you have just made!

 ## Unwrapping the GIFT

Resolving conflict is hard work, so try a sexual experience that says, "It *pays off* to work through the issues!" Get thirty one-dollar bills and toss them in the air over your bed. Have a "We're rolling in the money" sexual experience. Or pour sparkling cider into the small of each other's backs and "toast" the success of the conversation.

16

I Will Be Strong Where
You Are Weak

On my (Pam's) grandparents' sixtieth wedding anniversary, we traveled to Idaho to join in a huge celebration with friends and family. The morning of the party, Bill and I were sitting with my grandparents at the breakfast table. I said, "Well, Grandma and Grandpa, Bill and I travel all over the country giving marriage conferences. What's your secret? How did you make it sixty years together?"

They looked at one another, paused, then my grandmother tapped my grandfather's knee and said, "Pure grit and determination!"

Sixty years of pure grit and determination produced a deep, abiding love. What we learned from them is that a lifetime of love requires the ability to respect one another.

Grandpa respected the way Grandma ran the home, made the food, and served the community. Grandma respected her farmer/rancher husband for his handyman abilities and his wisdom. They each could have focused on the other's weaknesses: Grandpa was a little tight with his money. Grandma drank too much coffee and ate too little food. Grandpa should have gone to church more often. Grandma didn't want Grandpa to watch football with the sound on!

Oh sure, like everyone, they each had shortcomings. But they focused on what they appreciated about one another. They focused on how they could use their own personal strengths to build into the other's life to make it better. Their "I will be strong where you are weak" attitude carried them through until the very end.

Unfortunately, old age eventually robs us of our health. Giving for one another is a natural act at this stage because couples are so good at it by then! They've practiced selfless living and know the rewards of loving each other. But sacrifice is also hard, because giving at this point in life usually means caretaking for a spouse whose health is failing. It is always difficult to watch the one you love die.

Lifelong compassion, however, has its own priceless rewards. Grandma had been ill for several years. She and Granddad moved into my mother's home, where he lovingly cared for her. One night, she woke up and asked, "Gerald, could you hold me? I'm having a hard time breathing." And this night, like so many others, he took the lover of his life into his arms. Gently he held her and rocked her into the arms of heaven. She breathed her last breath knowing she was completely and totally loved.[1]

So what builds this kind of love, year after loving year? Your ability to handle differences in personality, makeup, strengths, and weaknesses. It is how you manage when you do not see eye to eye that will create a love that lasts.

Kim Buehlman, therapist and a University of Washington research coordinator with the Gottman Insititute, says,

> If you have a strong marital bond, you give your partner a break when times are tough. With a strong bond, even if a couple doesn't agree on something they find ways of avoiding destructive arguments because they really like each other and appreciate the differences. With a weak bond, you don't give respect and kindness to your partner. There is a lot more disagreement and a lot less friendship.[2]

So how can we develop the friendship and give our mates a break?

Get Perspective

You came into this marriage with some remarkable strengths. So did your spouse. And this is where the problems begin! At first, you are enamored with each other's abilities and idiosyncrasies. It doesn't take long, however, before the very things you love about each other become the exact things that irritate you.

There are three very common mistakes people make with their strengths that breed turmoil in intimate relationships

Mistake #1: They expect their spouses to have the same strengths they have.

Mistake #2: They focus more energy trying to overcome their weaknesses than they do trying to maximize their strengths.

Mistake #3: They try too hard to be good at what their spouses are best at.

Without a doubt, one of the hardest traits to develop as a married couple is unity. We all know couples who have been married for a long time, are very much in love, and work well together. We also all know of couples who don't appear to even like each other anymore. The difference between couples who love for a lifetime and those who have short-lived marriages is not talent or luck. The difference is the attitude that considers the relationship more important than the individuals involved.

A Strategy for Unity

The apostle Paul understood as well as anyone the possibility of unity among people who don't deserve it. At one point in his life, he was the enemy of God, but he grew to be one of the greatest champions of the gospel. There was a time when the church would not even allow him in its midst, yet he grew to be one its most beloved disciples. In Romans 15:1, he shared his formula for developing an attitude of unity: "We who are strong ought to bear with the failings of the weak" (Rom. 15:1).

In the movie *The Guardian*, we encounter a fascinating contrast between remarkable strength and surprising weakness in the same man. Jake Fisher and Billy Hodge are in training to be Coast Guard rescuers.

The relationally confident Jake was trying to coach his friend in the ways of women when the following conversation took place:

Jake Fischer: You gotta make a move!

Billy Hodge: I can't. I get nervous.

Jake Fischer: You're tellin' me you can jump outta helicopters but you're afraid to go talk to a girl?

Billy Hodge: Uh . . . pretty much, yeah.

We often feel this way in the battle of the sexes. Our relationships are risky, irritating, and irresistible. We are fascinated and frustrated with one another at the same time.

Isn't it amazing how strong you are at some things and how inept you are at others? Each of us is remarkably talented in some areas of life, but none of us is complete. As a result, we need a team of people around us to fill the gaps we leave behind.

One of my (Bill) favorite movies is the original *Rocky*. As Rocky's interest in the young pet shop clerk Adrian grows, her brother, Paulie, begins to question his intentions.

"Hey Rocky, what are you doing with my sister?"

Rocky's answer is one of the most insightful evaluations of marriage on the planet, "She has gaps. I have gaps. Together we fill gaps."

Rocky intensifies the theme in the sequel *Rocky Balboa*. Rocky is trying to advise his son, who is having a difficult time discovering who he is and what he should do with his life:

The world ain't all sunshine and rainbows. It is a very mean and nasty place and it will beat you to your knees and keep you there permanently if you let it. You, me, or nobody is gonna hit as hard as life. But it ain't how hard you hit; it's about how hard you can get hit, and keep moving forward. How much you can take, and keep moving forward. That's how winning is done.

Now, if you know what you're worth, then go out and get what you're worth. But you gotta be willing to take the hit, and not pointing fingers saying you ain't where you are because of him, or her, or anybody. Cowards do that and that ain't you. You're better than that!

You two are better than that too. You can choose to focus on a winning plan that maximizes your strengths as individuals instead of dwelling on a losing plan that magnifies your weaknesses. Pam and I have discovered that we do much better when we have a healthy respect for both the strengths *and* the weaknesses we bring to our relationship. I have always been in charge of home and car repairs because I am good with my hands. Pam has always been in charge of our family schedule because she is so much better than I am at juggling the details of our lives.

Gaps to Fill

If you expect your spouse to be strong all the time, you will be disappointed and experience conflict on a regular basis. If, on the other hand, you make room for each other's weaknesses and determine to fill the gaps in one another's lives, you will be amazed at how much better your life together is.

That was the point Paul was making in Romans 15:1. We make up for each other's weaknesses and please one another so we can be built up to be like Christ. This is Paul's take on what encouragement means: the Greek word for "encourage" is *parakaleo*, which means "to be called alongside." An encourager is one who is called alongside of another individual to help him become all that God wants him to be. An encourager will:

- Gently prod a loved one forward.
- Jump in and help when it is appropriate to do so.
- Back off when it is best for this person to pursue a specific step of growth alone.
- Confront a loved one when he is heading in a destructive direction.

- Provide consistent words of affirmation.

On our own, we don't possess the ability to influence others to the level we know is necessary, but we are not limited by our abilities. Encouragement is a powerful act because it puts us in partnership with the Holy Spirit. In John 14:16–17, we read, "And I will ask the Father, and he will give you another Counselor to be with you forever—the Spirit of truth." When Jesus referred to the Holy Spirit as "counselor," he used the word *paraclete* or "the one who is called alongside." In other words, the Holy Spirit is the ultimate encourager! He has been called alongside your spouse to bring out the best in him or her.

When you make the same commitment, you enter a partnership with the third person of the Trinity. You have help to provide to your spouse and your spouse has help to provide to you. When you pull together with the Holy Spirit to encourage one another, your influence on each other is truly supernatural.

Let us illustrate how this has played out in our relationship:

Bill's Strengths	How Bill's Strengths Have Helped Our Marriage
Careful and Analytical	Our finances are more organized, Pam's writing is proofread and edited well.
Good listener	Pam feels valued.
Talented with building and fixing things	We have built a home and remodeled two. We have consistently had nicer homes than we could otherwise afford.
Calm	Our parenting decisions are well balanced.

Bill's Strengths	How Bill's Strengths Have Helped Our Marriage
Talented in making complicated concepts simple	We have developed some innovative ministry concepts that have formed the foundation of an effective ministry.

Pam's Strengths	How Pam's Strengths Have Helped Our Marriage
Energetic and socially gifted	We have had a lot of fun.
Talented as a networker	We have an abundance of speaking opportunities.
Big thinker	Bill is living a bigger life than he would have on his own.
Proactive as a parent	Our kids have always looked ahead in life and have a good idea of who they are as individuals.
Creativity	Our life is always filled with options.

Bill's Weaknesses	How Pam Has Helped with this Weakness
Gets stressed when responsible for too many things	Pam has taken on responsibility for the areas that require multitasking (family schedule, speaking schedule, family birthdays, Christmas lists, etc.).
Shy	Pam has opened doors of opportunity for Bill.

Bill's Weaknesses	How Pam Has Helped with this Weakness
Timid when it comes to goals	Pam has helped Bill write goals every year they have been married. She encourages Bill to consider bigger goals.
Overcommits to helping people	Pam helps Bill decide the priority of each person's needs.

Pam's Weaknesses	How Bill Has Helped with this Weakness
Feels the need to control what she is involved with	Bill has helped her set priorities and decide on responsibilities based on the Bible, rather than her family of origin's expectations.
Overconfident	Bill has helped Pam make decisions based on God's leading rather than just the impulses of her heart.
Financially optimistic and overly generous	Bill manages the budget.
Feels slighted when people don't cooperate with her plan	Bill helps Pam evaluate people's involvement based on their responsibilities rather than on her agenda.

STOP Now it's your turn. Take time to make and fill in your own charts so you can decide together how you will make both your strengths and weaknesses work for you as a couple.

Shift to See How the Irritation Is Good for You

You've probably discovered that the things you loved most during your dating days can also be the very things that drive you crazy now. Instead of getting irritated, try to remember why you fell in love with your mate. See if it is one of his or her "great traits" that is now bugging you. If you can identify the positive (that is currently buried under the negative), you will be able to reconnect to him or her emotionally. For example:

Negative: He just changed plans on you midstream.

Positive: He is spontaneous so life is more fun!

Negative: She got angry because you were ten minutes late.

Positive: She is very organized and efficient with her time.

Sometimes it is just a matter of shifting your perspective so you can remember the reason you love your spouse so much!

While it's true that the things you love about each other are the very things that irritate you, it can also be true that the irritating trait is actually a benefit to you. I (Bill) love the fact that Pam is creative. We have had a lot of fun together. At the same time, it drives me crazy that she puts things away creatively in the kitchen, in the closets, and in the garage. She values creative expression so much that any comment I make about wanting things to be in better order feels like an insult to her.

I (Pam) love the fact that Bill is precise about things in life. It has helped in our financial management, the maintenance of our cars, and the ability to see commitments through to completion. But when he edits my writing, I have a hard time not taking it personally. When he comments on my driving or the way I keep the checkbook, it can easily trigger my worst self-talk.

Your most frequent arguments will be over the traits you most value in one another. Therefore, most of your disagreements hold the potential to remind you of the very thing that most attracts

244 The First Five Years

you to one another. The paradigm shift that can really help is to figure out how that irritating trait is actually something that is beneficial to you, your love, and your life together.

"Flip" Your Perspective

Every couple gets in conversational binds from time to time. When an emotional need sidetracks a conversation, you can recapture it by using passwords. Passwords are words or phrases you agree on that allow you to get back on track. They can be humorous or nostalgic statements that have special meaning to both of you. They are statements that remind you this relationship is important and that you are committed to making it work. They are statements that will break the ice of stalemated conversations because you have agreed ahead of time that they will. Passwords are like a pancake turner: when you make pancakes, when the batter begins to bubble, it signals it is time to flip the pancake. If you don't turn it quickly, one side gets burned. In the same way, when frustrations over idiosyncrasies begin to bubble up, this signals it is time to flip your perspective. Remember the old-and-true adage: opposites attract. We fell in love because our mates balance us out.

If you are spontaneous, you need a calm and focused spouse. If you are a couch potato, you probably fell in love with a life-of-the-party type. If you are a type A worker, you need someone who will take you down a notch and bring a little serenity. If you are easygoing, you might need someone to kick you in the pants and get you going!

But even if you fell in love with a person who balances you out, when that irritation occurs, you need to flip from a focus on the negative irritation and shift to the other side and remember why you first fell in love.

Early in our marriage, Bill took note that humor really helped when I would get overdramatic or melancholy. One of our passwords became a really bad joke Bill would perform from the original *Rocky* movie: "Yo, Pam! You know what you get when you tap a turtle on the back? Shell-shocked! Get it? Shell-shocked!" It would always make me laugh. We used it so often that sometimes he would just tap his wrist a certain way and I'd know he was talking about that turtle! Now, either of us can, in the middle of some really intense argument (the ones that are really over nothing of substance but maybe personality clashes and preference), say, "Yo!" or ask "What do ya get when ya tap a turtle?"

Whenever one of us uses this phrase, it makes us laugh, but it also is a compliment to the creativity and humor that we appreciate in each other. I (Bill) have found a new way to appreciate Pam in an area that used to leave me feeling as if the dots didn't connect.

The keys to a good password are:

- It reminds you of a good memory in your life together.

- It makes you laugh together.

- You agree on it. Phrases like "Suck it up" or "Get over it" are not good ideas for passwords.

STOP Try this exercise to find a password. List each of your favorite commercials. One couple discovered that they both liked Hallmark commercials so their password became "We care enough to send the very best." By saying this, the couple felt they were also saying to each other, "I'm trying to say it right. I want to, but it just isn't coming out like a greeting card. Can we try again?"

List your favorite cartoons or jokes. Humorous words are effective passwords. One couple thought their personalities were opposite. She was quieter and he was like the Warner Brothers' Roadrunner—always running one hundred miles per hour. So their password became, "Beep, beep!" That meant "Slow down. Don't try to fix me—listen to me."

List favorite movies or books. One couple selected the line, "I'm just no good without you" from a favorite Robert Redford

246 The First Five Years

movie; another had a line from a children's book: "Sorry, it is just a terrible, horrible, no good, very bad day."

Inside jokes that made you laugh during a horrible situation work the best. Maybe you've been through some hard circumstance and you can think of the line that broke the mood. What are some of your inside jokes?

Pressure Turned Positive

Sometimes it isn't your perspective on your spouse that needs to shift, but rather your view of the circumstance. Early in our marriage, when life got really stressful, Bill and I created stress managing games so we could stay emotionally connected and navigate through rough circumstances or daily hassles. Bill began the first game. On one particularly stressful day, he said, "I'd rather be stressed and married to you than lying on the very best beach in Hawaii." This began the "I'd rather be" compliments. A few of our favorites are:

- I'd rather be busy with you than resting with any other woman.

- I'd rather be eating at McDonald's with you than dining with any of the Fortune 500 men.

The other game is one we do when we are so stressed that we just need a break from the conflict or stressful circumstance. We take a walk and we play the "I can outinspire you game." We will hold hands and walk. The goal is to think of any inspiring saying, verse, or quote and say them back and forth. The conversation might sound like this:

- Bill, we can do all things through Christ who gives us strength.

- Pam, that is true if we first seek to understand, then be understood.

- Bill, that's so true, so it's especially important that I try to walk a mile in your shoes.

It is corny—but that's the point. The quotes, verses, and inspiring lines from T-shirts, refrigerator magnets, and famous people keep things lighter and brighter. The walk sends endorphins into the system and when you return to the conversation, you are in a better mood and you have a better perspective. Sometimes we can't change circumstances, and we don't always want to change our spouses, so the best thing to change is our attitude!

• • •

More than anything, your attitude is what will cement your love. Our mentor in marriage ministry, Jim Conway, surveyed couples who had long-lasting, happy marriages for his book, *Traits of a Lasting Marriage*, and you know what the most vital trait was to them? Those with happy, long-term marriages *decided* they wanted a happy, long-term marriage. Love is a decision. Love is a choice. Love is an action verb. Decide to give the GIFT of love you have learned about in these pages every day—and years from now you might find yourself sitting someplace liked the golden sands of Hawaii—on your golden anniversary. Enjoy the gift!

The GIFT

Create a refrigerator magnet to encourage your mate. Write a motto, a clever saying, a personalized verse that will remind him or her of your love. Create a fun reminder of your mate's strength.

Unwrapping the GIFT

Create your own reward system in the bedroom. Write down rewards you know your spouse would like to receive from you on little pieces of paper, then tape them to the backs of gold medals, blue ribbons, or on the bottoms of little trophies. Or use his or her favorite hobby or interest to set the stage for a unique reward ceremony. Think of the most creative way you can to thank your spouse for using his or her strengths to benefit you and your relationship.

Appendix:
Monthly Budget Worksheet

Income

    Salaries:

    Other:

Total income:

Expenses

    Tithe:

    Taxes:

    Housing (all expenses, including rent or mortgage, insurance, upkeep, decorating, utilities):

    Groceries:

    Auto (car payments, gas, upkeep, insurance, tax, and license):

    Insurance (life, health, and any other insurance):

    Debt (all debt, excluding mortgage and monthly minimum payments):

    Entertainment/recreation (eating out, tickets, video rental, any other activity, plus a monthly vacation savings amount):

Work expenses (child care costs; any professional expenses):

Clothing (list a monthly dollar figure for each family member):

Savings/retirement:

Medical expenses (any copayments, medical or dental bills not covered by insurance, monthly cost of prescriptions and over-the-counter medications):

Miscellaneous (personal care needs—haircuts, cosmetics, dry cleaning, personal allowance for each family member, reimbursed ministry expenses, gifts, educational costs, hobbies, postage, photos, magazines):

Total expenses:

Subtract expenses from income:

If income exceeds expenses, plan how to invest the surplus. If expenses exceed income, plan some quick action to cut expenses, raise income, or both. As newlyweds, we were taught this ditty:

If your outgo exceeds your income, your upkeep will become your downfall.

Notes

Introduction

1. John M. Gottman and Robert W. Levenson, "The Timing of Divorce: Predicting When a Couple Will Divorce over a 14-Year Period," *Journal of Marriage and the Family* 62 (August 2000): 737–745; http://www.gottman.com/research/abstracts/detail.php?id=3.

2. Drs. Bill Maier and Julianna Slattery, "The First Five Years" broadcast CD, Focus on the Family, Colorado Springs, 9 October 2006.

Chapter 2

1. Bill and Pam Farrel, *Men Are Like Waffles, Women Are Like Spaghetti* (Eugene, OR: Harvest House, 2001).

2. Ibid.

3. http://queenysobsessions.yuku.com/forum/viewtopic/id/737.

Chapter 3

1. "New Hope for PMS," *Vegetarian Times*, http://www.findarticles.com/m0820/n247/20380025/p1/article.jhtml.

2. John Eldredge, *Wild at Heart* (Nashville, TN: Thomas Nelson, Inc., 2001), 3–5.

3. *Harper's* (October 1998), as cited on PreachingToday.com.

Chapter 5

1. Amanda Groulx, "Thrusting Your Way to Better Health," The Eye Opener Online, February 7, 2006, http://www.theeyeopener.com/storydetail.cfm?storyid=2589.

2. George Barna, "People's Faith Flavor Influences How They See Themselves," Barna Research online, August 26, 2002, www.barna.org/cgi-bin/PageCatagory.asp?PressReleaseID=5.

Chapter 7

1. http://www.jumbojoke.com/hold_me_94.html.

2. Paul Byerly, "Physiology of the Male Sex Drive," The Marriage Bed Web site, http://www.themarriagebed.com/pages/biology/male/malephysiology.shtml.

3. I (Bill) will always be indebted to John Eldredge for expressing this theme throughout his book *Wild at Heart*.

Chapter 8

1. Family Safe Media, quoted on the Blazing Grace Web site, http://www.blazinggrace.org/pornstatistics.htm.

2. Forrest Research Report, 2001, ibid.

3. Testimony by Daniel Weiss at the May 19, 2005, Summit on Pornography, Focus on the Family Web site: http://www.family.org/socialissues/A000001158.cfm.

4. "The War Within" *Leadership Journal*, Fall 1984, 41, as quoted in Bill and Pam Farrel and Jim and Sally Conway, *Pure Pleasure* (Downer's Grove, IL: Intervarsity Press, 1994) 106.

5. *Infosearch* CD-ROM (Colorado Springs, CO: Navpress Software, 1987–1991).

6. Kenny Luck, Pastors.com, quoted on the Blazing Grace Web site, http://www.blazinggrace.org/pornstatistics.htm.

7. "Romance Fiction: Have We Got a Story for You," http://www.storyforu.com/stats.htm.

8. Ibid.

Chapter 11

1. Carrie Gordon Earl, "What We Did Not Know: The Aftermath of Thirty Years of Legal Abortion," Focus on the Family Web site, http://www.family.org/socialissues/A000000368.cfm.

2. Adapted (condensed) from the brochure *When Does Life Begin?*: http://www.mccl.org/stages4.htm; also National Right for Life brochure: http://www.mccl.org/credits.htm; and from NRL Web site "Fetal Development," 7 January 2003: http://www.w-cpc.org/fetal1.html; cross-referenced with medical sites: http://www.pregnancy.org/pregnancy/fetaldevelopment1.php#week6 http://baby2see.com/development/first_trimester.html.

3. http://www.nrlc.org/abortion/ASMF/asmf12.html.

4. http://www.nrlc.org/abortion/ASMF/asmf13.html.

5. Some of this contraception overview was gleaned from Dr. Ruth Westheimer, *Sex for Dummies* (Hoboken, NJ: Wiley Productions, 2007), 74–93.

6. Levonelle: http://www.levonelle.co.uk/output/Page51.asp.

7. Ibid.

8. Ibid.

9. http://www.nuvaring.com/Consumer/switch/aboutNuvaRing/index_flash.asp.
10. Levonelle: http://www.levonelle.co.uk/output/Page51.asp.
11. Ibid.
12. Ibid.
13. Ibid.
14. Ibid.
15. Ibid.
16. Ibid.

Chapter 12
1. T. Berry Brazelton and Stanley I. Greenspan, *The Irreducible Needs of Children* (Cambridge, MA: Perseus Publishing, 2000).
2. Heidi Brennan and Cathy Myers, "Beyond the Child Care Debate," http://www.familyandhome.org/policy/childcare_debate.html.
3. http://www.fosterclub.com/fyi3/fyi/stats/index.cfm.
4. http://en.wikipedia.org/wiki/Adoption_in_the_United_States.
5. http://www.blinkbits.com/bits/viewtopic/adoption_wikipedia?t=274818.

Chapter 13
1. Dr. Cleon L. Rogers and Cleon L. Rogers III, *The New Linguistic Key to the Greek New Testament* (Grand Rapids, MI: Zondervan, 1998), 539.

Chapter 15
1. Wit and Wisdom: http://witandwisdom.org/archive/20060620.htm.

Chapter 16
1. Parts of this story also appear in Bill and Pam Farrel, *Every Marriage Is a Fixer-Upper* (Eugene, OR: Harvest House, 2005), 181.
2. "UW Researchers Can Predict Newlywed Divorce, Marital Stability with 87 Percent Accuracy," 27 March 2000: http://uwnews.washington.edu/ni/article.asp?articleID=1863.

About the Authors

Bill and Pam Farrel are the bestselling authors of *Men Are Like Waffles, Women Are Like Spaghetti*. They are international speakers, relationship specialists, and the authors of over twenty-six books, including *Red-Hot Monogamy, Love, Honor, and Forgive,* and *10 Best Decisions a Parent Can Make.* Bill is a pastor at Shadow Mountain Community Church in Southern California. Pam is a frequent speaker for women's events and together, Bill and Pam run Masterful Living, an organization designed to bring practical insights to people's personal relationships. They have appeared on countless radio and television programs and are among the most sought-after speaking couples in the country. The Farrels are the parents of three and have recently welcomed a new daughter-in-law into the family. The Farrels make their home in San Diego, California. You can visit their Web site at www.farrelcommunications.com or call 800-810-4449.